Empowering
African-American
Males
to Succeed

A Ten-Step Approach
for Parents and Teachers

MYCHAL WYNN

EMPOWERING AFRICAN-AMERICAN MALES TO SUCCEED

A TEN-STEP APPROACH FOR PARENTS AND TEACHERS

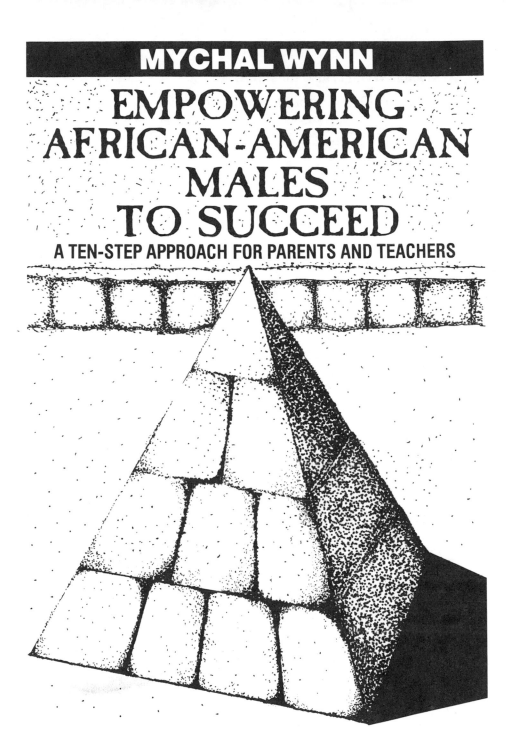

Rising Sun Publishing

South Pasadena, California

Mychal Wynn is also the author of

Don't Quit – Inspirational Poetry, 1990

FIRST EDITION 1992

Empowering African-American Males to Succeed.
Copyright ©1992 by Mychal Wynn

Complete lesson plans, parent workshops, teacher-staff development, video and audio tapes of this material are available through Rising Sun Publishing.

ISBN 1–880463–01–6

Rising Sun Publishing
1012 Fair Oaks Boulevard
South Pasadena, California 91030
(818) 799-1999

Printed in the United States of America.

Dedication

This book is dedicated to the young men whom we must empower to lead us into the future. I am thankful that the Lord has allowed my light to shine for you.

Acknowledgments

I thank my wife for her patience and understanding; my son for inspiring me to become the best father that I can be; my editor, Denise Mitchell Smith for her dedication to purpose; and the parents, educators, and all who are fighting the battle to save our young men. I've seen you in our schools and in our communities, with blood, sweat, and tears, scarred and bruised, yet determined to open the doors of opportunity so that our young men can achieve their potential. May God continue to bless and strengthen you!

The pain is in the eyes. Young Black men in their late twenties or early thirties living in urban America, lost and abandoned, aimlessly walking and hawking the streets with nothing behind their eyes but anger, confusion, disappointment and pain . . .

– Haki R. Madhubuti

Contents

Foreword

We must work together in identifying, analyzing, and resolving the multitude of problems confronting African-American males. The problems may be difficult and the recommended solutions may not necessarily be to our liking. Unfortunately, it is the debates over the solutions that often handcuff us into doing nothing or which cause us to implement only an abbreviated version of the solution that we proposed.

Empowerment is more than just a concept. It is an attitude where one feels capable of achievement, capable of resolving problems and successfully plotting and achieving direction in life.

Empowerment requires bringing spiritual forces to work on one's behalf to resolve those problems which appear insurmountable. The current crisis confronting the African-American family, in general, and the African-American male, in particular, is one which appears to be insurmountable and unsolvable by shear magnitude. We must work hands-on toward saving those within our circle of influence and through prayer, spiritually uplift those with whom we have no direct physical contact.

Empowerment requires that we bring all of our weapons to bear. We must apply ourselves mentally, physically, intellectually, emotionally, and spiritually to develop solutions to the multitude of challenges confronting us.

Having painfully endured Chicago's urban ghetto, I have gained first-hand insight into the daily fight for survival experienced by African-American men in America. I have experienced the pain, frustration, anger, and rage that consumes so many of our young men. The model that I've developed and the strategies that I propose cannot resolve all of the complex issues confronting African-American males. This book, and its associated workbook, is designed to offer a specific ten-step strategy for developing an empowered consciousness within African-American males. A consciousness that will enable our sons and our students to take control over their lives, accept responsibility for their actions, and gain the strength and courage to rebuild our communities. From boyhood to manhood, this book outlines a strategic plan for the classroom from Kindergarten through grade 12.

The ideas and strategies outlined in this book will reinforce and expand upon those already being used by many concerned parents and teachers. In workshops that I've presented throughout the country, parents and teachers have used the material contained in this book as a foundation from which to develop the working strategies needed to deal directly with the problems within their specific situation.

It is my desire that you embrace this book with the faith and self-assurance that you have the power to affect change. That your voice, in your school or community, speak out on behalf of our young men to develop the methods, systems, and support programs to ensure that they have the opportunity to succeed.

The Author

About the Author

Mychal Wynn grew up an only child in the urban ghetto of Chicago's infamous South Side. His father was a postal worker who provided for the family a clean, modest, one bedroom apartment. Mychal's many cousins lived in various Chicago land projects ranging from those located along Chicago's lake front to the State Street projects, spanning more than 20 city blocks. Although Mychal has become a nationally renowned author, workshop presenter, public speaker, educational and business consultant, he still has family trapped in the Chicago projects.

He learned to overcome what, for many, proved to be insurmountable obstacles. Mychal survived the gangs and violence confronting so many of our men growing up in the urban battlefields of America. A graduate, *Cum Laude*, of Boston's Northeastern University, Mychal has followed a successful corporate career path at multinational companies: Arthur Andersen & Company, IBM, and Transamerica.

Mychal is a Christian who adamantly believes that through Christ we all have the power to take control over our lives. And, he stands firmly on his conviction that "Where you come from does not determine where you're going, it only determines where you're beginning!"

His critically acclaimed book of inspirational poetry *Don't Quit*, has become a cornerstone of affirmation and inspirational teaching for thousands of trainers, teachers, parents, and business leaders throughout the country.

Mychal has been a workshop presenter; keynote speaker; and master of ceremonies for a multitude of community, civic, professional organizations, corporations, school districts, and churches. The workshop for the material contained in this book is among the most popular workshops that Mychal presents. All of his presentations are clear, concise, and effectively organized, leaving the audience with specific strategies for developing solutions to a variety of problems and issues.

Introduction

The African-American male is an endangered species. The 1990 U.S. Census Bureau figures show that African-American males have higher unemployment rates; lower labor force participation rates; lower high school graduation and college enrollment rates; while ranking first in incarceration and homicide as a percentage of the population.

The leading cause of death for African-American men between the ages of 15 and 24 is homicide. And, while representing only 6 percent of the population African-American men represent 49 percent of prison inmates. Only 4 percent of African-American males attend college, while 23 percent of those of college age are either incarcerated, on probation, or in prison. While African-American children nationwide comprise approximately 17 percent of all children in public schools, they represent 41 percent of all children in special education. Of the African-American children in special education, 85 percent of them are African-American males. African-American males, while comprising only 8 percent of public school students, represent the largest percentage, nationally, in suspensions (37 percent).

Nathan and Julia Hare, in *Bringing the Black Boy to Manhood: The Passage*, state:

> "The black race is like an unsteady palace, gigantic and ornate, teetering at its base while people gather around with cranes and complex machinery. The people squeal and squelch and prop the palace up, feverishly, pompously, working to repair it at its cracks and wobbly ceiling, when all the while the problem of the building's unsteadiness is a few missing bricks and broken mortar from its now all but invisible foundation."

Empowering African-American Males to Succeed embodies the spirit and mastery of pyramid building. The Great Pyramid at Gizeh represents one of the Seven Great Wonders of the World. This monument of architectural genius, designed and constructed by Africans, represents one of the most remarkable and extraordinary achievements in the history of mankind.

The design of the Great Pyramids of Egypt were divinely inspired; the blocks were constructed and laid into place by thousands of African hands. The construction of these pyramids, many of which took as many as thirty years to build, involved the collective effort of thousands of people working together. This clearly sets an example for us that extraordinary things are possible.

This book, through the spirit of pyramid building, lays each block into place for a strong foundation. Each following layer is laid into place purposefully as an integral part of a larger plan. The cement that holds these blocks together is the love, leadership, and sincerity needed to empower African-American males to succeed.

Jawanza Kunjufu, in *Countering the Conspiracy to Destroy Black Boys, Volume II,* states: "A major reason why Black boys are placed in special education is because many teachers don't appreciate the idea that children learn in different ways and they bond less with children who don't look like them. There are also many teachers who are AFRAID of Black boys."

New approaches to reach these young men are beginning as various school districts have begun experimental programs in which "All-African-American-Male" classrooms have been established. These classes are taught by African-American men who provide leadership and role models for their students. Such programs have been acknowledged by their founders as drastic means of reaching and teaching our young men.

Although our community has become increasingly frustrated over our schools' inability to educate African-American urban children, particularly our young men, we differ greatly in our opinions about such programs that separate our young men from the mainstream student body. Many believe that we should provide better training for our parents and teachers. Yet others believe that better leadership in our school systems will ensure that our young men are afforded a quality education in a supportive learning environment without separating them from the mainstream. Regardless of the strategy we choose to employ, we must agree that something needs to be done.

This book seeks to provide a clear and cohesive ten-step approach for empowering African-American males to succeed. It contains specific strategies that teachers and parents can implement in the classroom and at home.

If we want our young men to achieve a valuable and respectable place in society, we must empower them to think and to do for themselves in ways that are morally sound and socially acceptable.

If we want to increase the numbers of our young men enrolling in college; starting businesses; developing strong cohesive African-American families; and rebuilding our communities, we must empower them to make the necessary life-saving decisions.

If we want to decrease the numbers of our young men entering prisons; being placed upon the rosters of the hopeless and homeless; and losing their lives on the urban battlefields of America, we must empower them to believe that they can take charge of their lives and control their destinies.

The strategies, techniques, and exercises outlined in this book are so profoundly simple that it's scary. It's scary that these strategies and techniques are not commonplace in every school, home, and community concerned with the tragic plight of African-American men.

*Our people have made the mistake of confusing the
methods with the objectives. As long as we agree on
objectives, we should never fall out with each other
just because we believe in different methods or tactics
or strategy . . . We have to keep in mind at all times
that we are not fighting for integration, nor are we
fighting for separation. We are fighting for recognition
as free humans in this society.*

– Malcolm X

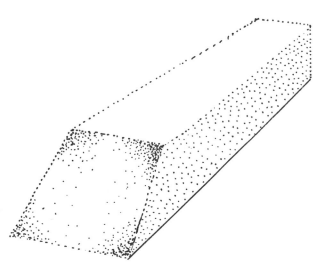

Block 1

CULTURAL UNDERSTANDING

A teacher is very much like a business consultant. During the fact-finding phase the consultant researches the people, culture, and goals of the organization. The consultant then identifies the problems and issues confronting the organization before recommending possible solutions. Teachers develop effective lesson plans and teaching strategies through an in-depth understanding of their students, their community, and the obstacles and issues that uniquely pertain to them. Even an understanding of these factors represents a moving target. Teaching strategies must change as people, communities, schools, and the times change.

In his 1933 publication, _The Mis-Education of the Negro_, Carter G. Woodson explained:

"Unless African-Americans receive an education befitting to their peculiar situation, they would never enter fully into the economic, political and social institutions in the United States of America. The mere imparting of information is not education, above all, the effort must make a man think and do for himself. The program for the uplift of the Negro in this country must be based upon a scientific study of the Negro from within to develop in him the power to do for himself. To educate the Negro we must find out exactly what his background is, how to begin with him as he is and make him a better individual of the kind that he is, instead of cramming the Negro's mind with what others have shown that they can do, we should develop his latent powers that he may perform in society a part of which others are not capable."

Asa Hilliard, in his foreword to Janice Hale-Benson's book *Black Children: Their Roots, Culture, and Learning Styles,* states: "A discussion of the growth, development, and cognition of the African-American child must take into account that culture is one of the greatest environmental variables. It is at this point that Western behavioral science has failed in the study of African-American children." Although many of the examples, exercises, and strategies contained in this book can be applied to all children, as Carter G. Woodson pointed out in 1933, and, as Asa Hilliard points out over a half century later, our strategies must take into account the culture and inherent differences of those whom we teach.

Wade Nobles, in *Infusion of African and African-American Content in the School Curriculum,* states: "When we look at the notion of culture and raise the question of accessing children to a core curriculum, we should be very clear that the core curriculum itself is cultural; and that the teaching methodology that we utilize in teaching the core curriculum is also cultural; and that the site leadership style is cultural, and that the guidance and counsel techniques are cultural, and that the instructional strategies are cultural, and that the school climate is cultural, and that ultimately the aim and purpose of education itself is cultural."

EXERCISE #1

1. Identify one young man in your classroom or if you're a parent, identify your son.

2. Write his name at the top of a blank sheet of paper.

3. Draw lines to divide the sheet into four parts.

4. Label the first area:

    ROLE MODELS

    (i.e., Athletes, Entertainers, Teachers, etc.).

5. Label the second area:

    FAMILY ENVIRONMENT

    (e.g., father at home, 2 brothers, sisters with children, etc.).

6. Label the third area:

    CULTURAL CHARACTERISTICS

    (i.e., latest styles, clothes, hair, etc.).

7. Label the fourth area:

    PERSONAL CHARACTERISTICS

    (e.g., low self-estccm, highly influenced by peer pressure, displays leadership skills, etc.).

8. Finally, write this young man's goal under his name at the top of the page. If he has never developed a goal for himself give him one.

Let's see how much we know about this young man.

1. Who are some of his role models?

2. What is his family structure and environment like?

3. What are some of his unique cultural characteristics?

4. What are some of his unique personal characteristics?

If you found yourself staring at your paper bewildered at how little you know about this young man, don't worry, you're in good company. At workshops throughout the country when seminar audiences perform this exercise, many parents, teachers, counselors, and administrators receive a wake up call! They realize how little they understand about the young men whom they are attempting to teach, raise, and motivate.

In urban communities across America, our young men are growing up on urban battlefields where they must make life-saving decisions daily. Our parents, teachers, administrators, and even African-American professionals who were raised in these same urban communities a decade or more before, are as unfamiliar with the issues and circumstances confronting our young men along the streets of our inner city communities, in our homes, and in the hallways of our schools as we were with our soldiers fighting in the jungles and rice fields of Vietnam.

One night Freddie and I were walking along Calumet Avenue on Chicago's South Side when suddenly two young men leaned out of a first floor tenement window. Less than six feet away one young man pointed a double-barrel shotgun at us and said, "Represent." This shotgun-wielding young man was asking us to proclaim our gang affiliation. This was a rite of passage. The correct response would allow these two thirteen year olds to pass unharmed. The incorrect response would send two more of our young men to a premature death.

Freddie immediately pounded his chest with his right fist and proclaimed, "Disciple thang." The shotgun-wielding young man responded, "Disciple thang, walk on." Freddie and I, at age thirteen, understood the community we were walking through; which gang controlled the turf; how to walk; and how to respond. These survival skills, in that instant, helped us to see fourteen.

The following are some of the cultural characteristics of our young men that may have been included on your list:

- High stress communities and households
- Athletically competitive
- Highly influenced by peer pressure
- Physically mature at an early age
- Role models are people who are recognized by peers, portrayed on mass media through television and radio
- Low self-esteem
- Low goals
- Low academic motivation
- Lacking positive peer and parental support
- Unbalanced diet
- Noisy home environment
- High energy and high spirited
- Enjoys rhythm, dance, and Rappin' (an oral tradition of communication)
- Humanistic
- Extended family and bonding is important (e.g., uncles, grandfathers, athletic teams, gangs)
- Highly influenced by latest clothes, shoes, and hair styles
- Experiences and uses profanity at early ages
- Verbally and physically aggressive
- Shorter attention span
- Less cooperative
- Larger and more sensitive ego
- Lacking physically accessible positive male role models
- Culturally distinctive speech ("Black English")

- Culturally distinctive style of walk ("The Walk")
- Culturally distinctive handshakes
- Uses nonverbal communication (e.g., hands, eyes, body language)
- Affinity toward team and group activities
- Illiterate or marginally literate family
- First-hand experience with violent crime
- Negative experience with law enforcement
- Friends, family members in gangs
- Family members in jail or on parole
- Family or family members on welfare
- Poverty or marginally poverty family
- Disorganized household
- Non-assertive or inarticulate parents
- Under or unemployed parents
- Powerless parents
- Substandard housing
- Lacking regular medical and dental care
- Transient family
- Family overload
- Non-academic home
- Family history of substance abuse
- Single parent household
- Many teenage pregnancies
- Community lacks cultural alternatives
- Community lacks esthetic values
- History of apathetic teachers
- Feels powerless to resolve many personal conflicts

A young man came into the classroom today angry. Some of the students said good morning and the young man snapped, "Get out of my face." The young man folded his arms, arched his eyebrows, and walked away. One of the young men came over to repeat his good morning and the young man raised his fist as he shouted, "Leave me alone."

This young man was uncooperative, angry, and potentially violent.

Was he from a single-parent home where his mother wasn't properly disciplining him? Or from an inner city, lower economic, physically-aggressive household? Had he witnessed substance abuse or been exposed to other types of physical or verbal abuse? Which is most nearly true?

Neither! This was my own son one morning at preschool. He was just having a bad day. Our young men represent the complete spectrum of American life. They come from every community, family background, economic status and social strata; from single-parent households to two-parent dual income households. Their parents range from little formal education to Ph.Ds. Many parents provide the love, leadership, and discipline to establish within our young men a clear understanding of expected behavior.

Our young men often develop and maintain a proper code of conduct at home. Yet, outside the home our young men share a subculture within the culture that bonds them together. That subculture is constantly evolving, yet it remains the same. Although the words have changed, the rituals of "The Dozens," "The Showdown," "Rappin'," and "The Walk" have remained the same for generations in our community. Understanding our culture, and understanding the uniqueness of each of our young men is the first step in teaching, raising, motivating, and empowering them to succeed.

7

EXERCISE #2

1. Have your young men fill out a sheet of paper listing: favorite foods, clothes, cars, sports, entertainers, politicians, recording artists, role models, dances, songs, places to live, teachers, etc.

2. Add to this list anything that you feel would give you greater personal insight (e.g., how he gets to school, what time he wakes up, if he eats breakfast, etc.).

3. Have him fill out another sheet of paper writing about the things that he most enjoys doing (e.g., fishing, dancing, playing basketball, watching TV, etc.).

4. Use these papers to gain greater insight into the personal differences and cultural commonality of these young men. Use this information to identify the types of things which motivates our young men personally and culturally.

5. Keep these sheets of paper and repeat the same exercise at the end of the school year.

As our young men grow, learn, gain confidence, self-esteem, and develop a more positive self-image, they will begin to identify new role models, expand their hobbies, and the things that they enjoy.

EXERCISE #3

1. Have your young men complete a one-page paper (e.g., narrative, rap, poem, etc.) for each of the following:

    a. What do I want to be?

    b. What does it mean to be a man?

    c. What does it mean to be a father?

    d. Who do I most admire and why?

2. Use these responses to stimulate a classroom or one-on-one discussion. Encourage your young men to share and articulate their feelings while being careful to keep the discussion positively focused, restricting laughter, mocking, and name-calling.

3. Keep these papers for now. Repeat this exercise after completing the other exercises in the pyramid.

Expanding our cultural understanding of our young men will enable us to gain a greater awareness of the "why" behind behavioral characteristics and how certain behavior is interwoven within the culture. Without understanding what conflicts and issues they are being confronted with daily in their homes and along the streets of their communities, we cannot develop a curriculum that is relevant to life as they see it. One of the instructional breakdowns in urban schools is relating discussions about African-American history and the achievements of African-American men to the current conflicts confronting our young men. The ongoing discussions of the vision and philosophies of such African-American men as Martin Luther King, Jr., Malcolm X, W.E.B. DuBois, Booker T. Washington, and Carter G. Woodson can provide our young men with a foundation from which to develop an understanding of the many issues that have led to the crisis within our communities. From this foundation they can begin to develop ideas and survival skills that will help them to place the daily life-threatening confrontations which they're experiencing in our communities and American society into a perspective that will allow them to make the necessary life-saving decisions.

Wade Nobles, regarding the role of culture in education, stated that, "Culture is to humans as water is to fish. It is our total environment. As such, education, as well as curriculum development, are cultural phenomena. Culture is as the nature of the water (i.e., salt vs . fresh vs. polluted) influences the reality (i.e., survivability) of particular types of fish, so too do different cultural systems influence the reality of particular groups of people." We must teach our young men that their speech, although non-standard is not inferior; that their dress, dance, music, food, and other cultural differences are just that, "differences," as they relate to other cultures.

The self-image of our young men can be irreparably damaged by teachers who view our young men as culturally disadvantaged. Their lessons and teaching methods communicate their feelings, and reinforce the idea that African-Americans cannot become successful in American society unless they discard their culture and adapt European customs and values. What's being communicated to our young men is, "Forget that stuff that you do at home and along the streets of your community. You can only become successful if you act, talk, and behave a certain way (the European way)!"

The Proficiency in English Program (PEP) of the Los Angeles Unified School District has made exemplary strides in helping teachers and parents to understand the concept of "Situational Appropriateness." By understanding the cultural characteristics of our young men and their communities, PEP Advisors help teachers and parents to understand that the "appropriateness" of European-American culture as it relates to survival within the larger society should not displace the "appropriateness" of African-American culture as it relates to survival within the African-American community. PEP teaches our young men to walk, talk, and behave in a manner that is appropriate for achieving success within certain dimensions of American society. However, our young men must continue to walk, talk, and behave a certain way to survive and remain bonded within the culture of the African-American community.

We must develop for our young men an Afrocentric curriculum at school, and a positive, encouraging, culturally rich environment at home. The classrooms and homes of our young men should have books and magazines written by, and about, African-Americans. Art and literature, positively portraying African-American men should fill our bookshelves and be displayed on our walls. Discussions and debates of the philosophies, literary works, educational, political, and professional achievements of African-American men should become a part of the daily curriculum. Newspaper and Magazine articles about successful African-American men should be placed into a scrapbook that chronicles the year keeping our young men focused and aware of our daily achievements.

We should encourage our young men to write letters to successful African-American authors, entrepreneurs, politicians, civil rights, and community leaders. Their self-image, and their awareness of networking, can be powerfully enhanced by our continuing encouragement that they have what it takes to become as successful as those they study. Those young men who don't have positive male role models at home can draw strength and courage from the achievements of those current day men they are discussing, researching, seeing in the media, and corresponding with.

We should expand our Career Day programs to include a discussion period with career presenters before they go into classrooms to prepare them to make their careers interesting. In addition to their careers they should discuss what they had to do to gain the opportunity to enter into their chosen fields. They should describe their diligence and determination; their ability to overcome such obstacles as racism, prejudice, and fear that enabled them to succeed. They should discuss how they endured, relating their personal experiences.

Presenters must be mobile, moving around the room and raising their energy levels. They should share some of their most frustrating and challenging situations both as a child and as an adult. They should relate their cultural experiences to the students so that our young men can identify with them. (E.g., What type of communities did they grow up in? Did they attend a Black College? Who inspired them to pursue excellence in their lives? If they could do it again what would they change in their lives?) Speaking to our young men in this way opens their minds to new opportunities. It makes new career possibilities more tangible from their perspective.

"The Dozens" is a ritualistic game believed to have originated in the African country of Nigeria. It was a tribal tradition that competing boys typically put down each other's father in this verbal game of one-upmanship to manhood. As a reflection of the absence of the father in many African-American homes, competing boys typically put down the mother instead.

"The Dozens" has also been called "Signifying and Rankin'." Today's Rap music has its roots in "The Dozens." The purpose of this game is to hurl verbal assaults sufficiently clever to be proclaimed the winner by one's peers. This game is generally played by two young men who hurl verbal insults at each other personally and about their lineage while a group of young men cheers them on (or more commonly know as instigate). If neither person gives in, the group eventually proclaims a winner. Occasionally, the game will result in a physical confrontation if one person is unable to withstand the level of insults. This, of course, is tantamount to weakness in the eyes of his peers.

To excel at this game, a young man must be able to communicate verbally through rhythm and rhyme; to think and respond quickly. He must be able to listen, focus, and pay close attention to what is being said so that he may counter with something stronger, funnier, and more clever that what's been said about him or his lineage. (In their vernacular: "Yo Mama.")

As a child growing up in Chicago, I played and lost at this game often. Being skinny, fair skinned, and having a short, stout mother gave my adversaries plenty of ammunition for the ensuing battle. It was common for my schoolmates to listen intently for another adult to say my mother's name, Ernestine. From then on, "Ernestine" always made a quick entrance into "The Dozens." I lost at the dozens so often that I was convinced until I entered college that being fair skinned clearly indicated that I lacked "soul."

Most teachers, particularly non-African-American teachers, demonstrate their lack of understanding of "The Dozens" by

13

attempting to ban this form of African-American male culture. Many will attempt to break up the game with threats of suspension or other forms of punishment. Others become afraid of our young men because of their intensity and boisterous behavior during the game, and will call security or other authority figures to break up the game. Few recognize, or are willing to accept this as part of our culture. If the game is banished from your classroom it simply finds its way into the bathroom, locker room, or onto the street corner.

Why not acknowledge the game and the verbal, thinking, and cognitive skills that are being developed? Why not acknowledge the sense of involvement and camaraderie exhibited by those observing the game, as well as the heightened sense of self-esteem by the young man proclaimed the winner by his peers?

EXERCISE #4

1. Find out who is; best at the dozens and challenge that person to a duel; but there's a new twist. The challenge is to say the most positive, encouraging, uplifting, supportive, and loving things. Start the game and get other young men involved. Encourage boisterous instigation of a positive nature. Notice the intensity, passion, and spirit of our young men as they join in.

2. Discuss the history of "The Dozens." Discuss with them the tradition in ancient Africa. Tell them how the young men of the village would say things about each other and their fathers as a rite of passage into manhood.

3. Give them an assignment to write a "Dozens" about themselves, proclaiming their greatness, cultural achievements, royal heritage, and future success.

4. Expand the discussion to include why we say such negative things to each other as:

   "I hate you."

   "You make me sick."

   "I can't stand you."

   "You're stupid."

   "You're ugly."

   "I wish you were dead."

5. Play a game where each person makes a positive one-line statement about the person next to him.

6. Expand the discussion about the effect that powerful, life-giving words have on ourselves and others.

7. Have them close their eyes and say a positive one-line statement about themselves.

8. Move through the group while their eyes are closed. Place your hands on their shoulders as you move along so that they can hear and feel your support. Reassure them that you care.

Jawanza Kunjufu, in *Countering the Conspiracy to Destroy Black Boys, Volume II*, says that "When a Black boy looks at the female teacher with a look of defiance, I call this the SHOW-DOWN."

My son is two years old and is already familiar with the Show-down. There are times when he doesn't get his way, for whatever reason, and will stop whatever he's doing, fold his arms defiant-ly, arch his eyebrows, and stare directly into your eyes. At two years old, my son is more hilarious than intimidating. But what about the young man in your classroom? The young man, who by his posture, has defiantly assumed authority; the student who has issued a personal challenge to you! The showdown is a cultural challenge. My son issues it to my wife, and our young men issue it to their classroom teachers.

Our young men learn very early in our urban communities that a person must either be physically strong, mentally quick, quick-of-foot, or have some "wolf tickets to sell!" Without one or more of these attributes, it is difficult to survive. The showdown not only occurs in the classroom. Our young men issue the chal-lenge on every basketball court and football field; in every schoolyard and classroom.

I'll never forget transferring to a new school in the seventh grade. This was a private middle school in Chicago. Located in the heart of the inner city on Chicago's South Side, it had an all-Black student body. The male students wore white or light blue shirts with black or dark blue slacks. The girls wore white or light blue blouses with plaid skirts. So naturally, the students stood out in the community as they walked to and from school. The African-American males would experience the showdown in the classroom as well as on the journey to and from school.

I was prepared for the showdown each day that I left my neighborhood to journey through other neighborhoods to get to school. Some dude would "get in my face" asking for money.

Someone else would ask what gang I represented. Someone else would accuse me of seeing some young lady in the neighborhood.

Any African-American young man growing up in the ghetto of Chicago's South Side, or worse, Chicago's West Side, had to know how to respond to the showdown. Sometimes you fought; sometimes you ran; sometimes you "sold wolf tickets." The showdown is a rite of survival! It's an urban rite of passage.

For teachers, who don't understand our culture, the showdown can be devastating for them, and ultimately, for our young men:

> "Clyde sat there, defiantly, his arms folded staring at the teacher. Most of our substitutes were afraid to call on Clyde so they attempted to ignore him. This only encouraged Clyde to exert more control as he lost respect for the teacher. He became openly disobedient. He raised his desktop, ignored requests to open his book, and taunted the girls in the classroom. Eventually, when the teacher could ignore Clyde no longer, she typically would waste a great deal of the class's time: 'Clyde don't do this, Clyde don't do that, Clyde please sit down!' "

The teacher had obviously lost the battle and the class was out of control. Even in a private school, the teacher left this assignment with lowered self-esteem and probably a negative opinion of African-American children, our young men in particular. Any future showdowns will probably bring similar results. The teacher will probably convey her opinion of African-American males to anyone willing to listen. She will probably mention Clyde to all the teachers in the teacher's lounge. Clyde's future teachers will be ready for him!

As a young man I engaged in the showdown as a release from boredom. I generally caught on to my subjects very quickly. As I lost interest in the class, I would begin to doodle, draw, write poetry, or respond with what I thought were witty answers to questions! I was always put out of class for one reason or another. This was just what I wanted! I had won the battle against the teacher. I'll never forget the nicest Nun who passed me each day in the hallway outside my classroom and responded, "Mychal, I see you're holding up the wall again." Although I spent hours each day leaning against the wall in the hallway, I was still one of the top ten students in my class. But, how much was lost because no one thought it important to develop a teaching strategy that would capture my attention?

The showdown is a cultural test of strength. "This is my domain; my class; this is where I rule; you can't make me learn." I have experienced in the classrooms where I've worked with our young men, and from the comments made by teachers in my workshops, that the showdown is a challenge that can be won by the teacher through bonding. Our children are humanistic. Our young men, particularly, want to be loved. They want to feel important and valuable to their peers, teachers, and parents. Our young men want to be respected and they will respect only those who demand their respect. The showdown is a test of "Will you respect me? Will you demand my respect? Will you love me? Will you motivate me to learn?"

Many teachers, particularly substitute teachers, don't understand the showdown and depending upon their own self-esteem, personal confidence, and whether or not they have a natural tendency to be afraid of our young men, don't respond in a way that establishes the foundation for discipline in the classroom — discipline that is established on the foundation of cultural understanding. When our young men don't feel loved or respected, when they're not motivated to learn, they exhibit anger and rebellion toward the teacher. This further alienates or frightens the teacher and no learning is achieved.

Teachers who lose control of their classrooms on the first day spend most of their time thereafter attempting to establish discipline. All of our children suffer. Many parents and teachers attempt to discipline by intimidation. They feel that by being bigger and stronger they can force our young men to behave. This is building a house on sand! When these young men grow bigger and stronger, guess who becomes the intimidator? We must develop a bond of mutual respect with our young men where disciplined, well-mannered behavior is expected and rewarded. To effectively teach our young men we must understand their culture. They will respond to and respect a confident, assertive tone rather than a weak plea for them to behave.

Avoid the showdown by establishing the foundation of class-room discipline early. When confronted with the showdown, be forceful yet loving in your tone. Establish your authority!

Make it clear that certain behavior is unacceptable.

Effective teachers understand the importance of bonding with our young men. When someone is unruly, they may continue their classroom discussion while positioning themselves near the student.

Once there they simply place their hand on the young man's shoulder. This says "I know you want my attention; I'm not afraid of you; I care about you!"

*We realize that our future lies chiefly in our own
hands. We know that neither institution nor friends
can make a race stand unless it has strength in its
own foundation; that races like individuals must
stand or fall by their own merit; that to fully succeed
they must practice the virtues of self-reliance,
self-respect, industry, perseverance, and economy.*

– Paul Robeson

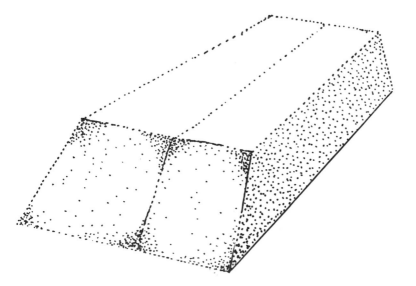

Block 2

MUTUAL RESPECT
CHARACTER DEVELOPMENT

Our classrooms can no longer begin and end with the simple tasks of teaching reading, writing, and arithmetic. Elizabeth Hood, in _Educating Black Students: Some Basic Issues,_ points out that "Urban schools frequently fail to encourage the urban child to become interested in leadership because the curriculum does not include an adequate number of co-curricular activities. Many teachers and administrators assume that the Black child's primary educational needs are discipline and the three R's. They fail to understand that the heightened sense of power and self-esteem which stem from involvement in meaningful activities will motivate the child to become more self-directed and more anxious to improve his basic skills." We must take a holistic approach to teaching our young men in which we study and teach the total person.

Our young men must be taught of their responsibilities to themselves, their families, and their communities and held accountable for their actions. They must be taught self-respect and respect for other people and their property.

We must develop our home, community, church, and school environments to develop, encourage, and nurture leadership skills and character within our young men. We must encourage a standard of behavior and code of conduct and not allow disrespect

25

and ill-mannered behavior in the classroom or at home. The development of these skills is as important and are essential to any academic study.

Frederick Douglass stated: "It is vain that we talk of being men, if we do not the work of men. We must become valuable to society in other departments of industry than those servile ones from which we are rapidly being excluded. We must show that we can do as well as they. When we can build as well as live in houses; when we can make as well as wear shoes; when we can produce as well as consume wheat, corn and rye—then we shall become valuable to society."

Our young men are seldom interested in working at McDonald's or in the prospects of simply getting a good job. But they are interested in the material success of owning a McDonald's. Our young men are rarely interested in working at the checkout counter or in the stock room at the local grocery store. But they are interested in the prestige that comes from owning a grocery store. We must teach mutual respect and reinforce character development within a framework that helps them to understand that their character, integrity, diligence, and determination bears a direct relationship with realizing their dreams and aspirations. In order to do this we must understand their dreams and aspirations.

Carter G. Woodson stated: "When you hear a man talking, then, always inquire as to what he is doing or what he has done for humanity? Old men talk of what they have done, young men of what they are doing, and fools of what they expect to do." Our young men must be taught that whatever they do individually reflects on the community as a whole; that they are in fact the lifeblood of the community. We must work diligently to develop bonding between students and teachers, students and themselves, and our young men and the community around them. This bonding is a vital part of strengthening the African-American community. This holistic approach to teaching our young men

26

requires that we integrate discussions about character, morality, integrity, and diligence into our history, math, and science lessons.

What good is served if we teach our young men math when they don't have the diligence, determination, or integrity to become a CPA? What good is served if we teach them science and they don't have the character to enter a medical school to pursue a career as a doctor?

In laying our first block we identified that our young men gravitate toward team sports and group activities. Subsequently, our young men develop an early understanding of the concept of teamwork. Using this natural gravitation toward team sports and group activities, peer pressure can influence and reinforce positive values within our classrooms. The more we encourage our young men to engage in discussions and to express their opinions about these concepts the greater the possibility of positive values being adopted by their peers and the greater the potential of our young men becoming empowered with these values.

We cannot develop character where there is no discipline! The National Education Association sites discipline as the number one problem in American classrooms. The undisciplined student is lacking in one of the key elements needed for setting, focusing upon, and achieving goals. The undisciplined classroom cannot establish the environment for learning. Establishing a disciplined environment, and teaching our young men self-discipline requires expanding upon our cultural understanding.

Elizabeth Hood, in *Educating Black Students: Some Basic Issues,* describes the experience of a Black Administrator with three seventh grade Black males expelled from a classroom:

> I said to these three small but energetic boys "This is the third time in a week that you three have been sent to the

office from Miss J's class. What is the problem with you in Miss J's class?"

One of the boys responded "Miss J just picks on us. The whole class makes noise in that lady's room. She doesn't know how to make us behave. All the kids act up in that room. She doesn't like us three, so she sends us to the office to try to scare the other kids."

"You do get along well in your other classes?" I asked.

"Well, Ma'am, it's like this," the smaller of the three joined in, "We do all right when the teachers really get us when we get out our seats and make noise. We don't do nothing wrong in those classes. No Ma'am."

The outcome of the battle was always decided on the first day the students entered the class. If the teacher failed to "make them" at that initial encounter, the battle was over and the teacher the loser.

Culturally, many of our young men respect only those who enforce discipline.

This situation is repeated too often throughout our schools. Our young men respecting only those who make them behave. Yet, without understanding our culture, many teachers never become successful at making them behave. If we successfully establish the foundation of cultural understanding, we will begin to understand the importance that our young men place on bonding, mutual respect, and love. When the teacher succeeds at bonding and establishing the foundation of mutual respect, it is easy to discuss, in love, the potential problem areas with our young men. The goal of discipline is not to "make them" behave, but to encourage them to think and to establish self-discipline.

Our young men are humanistic and long for bonding. If we bond with them, our job will become more fulfilling and our goal of establishing a disciplined classroom will be more easily achieved. In establishing classroom discipline, the teacher should discuss how personal discipline relates to achieving their goals. The classroom discussion should help our young men to understand how a misbehaving student interferes with personal goal achievement, classroom goal achievement, and the teacher's goal achievement.

Our young men have no problem disciplining themselves when they have established goals on the basketball court or football field. They will study for days on end until they have mastered the latest rap song. They will practice for weeks until they have mastered the latest dance steps. Teachers and parents want to have pride in their children. There is no greater feeling for a parent than to show off a handsome, strong, well-mannered son. Yet, an undisciplined classroom is no worse than a parent with a single disobedient child (there are simply more of them). We must empower our young men by establishing the proper foundation of courtesy, pride, dignity, and a proper code of conduct. Sound simple enough?

My wife is still working her way through building the foundation for our son. Generally, you will find my wife meticulously dressed, her nails polished and manicured, her hair neat and very stylish. During her professional career, she has successfully provided counseling and career guidance for hundreds of employees. She has developed good people skills and is the epitome of organization.

One day my wife came home frazzled! She came into the house with her hair standing all over her head, several broken fingernails, her clothes soiled, and a run in her stockings, decreeing: "I'm never taking your son to the store with me again. He just acted like an absolute ninny! I've never been so embarrassed in my life. He didn't want to do anything that I told him, he started crying in the store because he wanted me to buy him a beach ball, then he wanted to open some candy. He wouldn't sit in the shopping cart, then he wanted me to pick him up, and to go from bad to worse he started crying and throwing a fit in the checkout line. When I tried to calm him down, he called me stupid! At that point I was so worn out that I just left the groceries and came home." After all of this, our two year old son strolls innocently through the door, oblivious to his mother's distress.

I rarely experience this type of behavior with our son. The next day I took him to the store (to reclaim our groceries), together with his four year old cousin who has a reputation in the family of being difficult. The three of us spent the entire day together in various situations before returning home. While at home, I did some work on my computer while they played in the yard. On other occasions, my son and I have spent the entire day together, in various situations, and have never had any problems.

There is a difference in the way in which an African-American male child responds to a woman and in the way he responds to a man. He will often test women until they demand his respect. And even then he will occasionally challenge them. Our young men are typically unresponsive to a woman's voice when instructed the first time. Often a mother or teacher will make the same request several times before our young men respond. They establish in their minds how much they can get away with. They may not respond until the mother or teacher is screaming and threatening them. Our young men have coolly pushed their mothers and teachers to the end of their rope before responding to their instructions.

My wife understands that no matter how tired she is or how busy she may be, when she asks our son to do something she has to follow with some form of discipline if he doesn't respond immediately. She has to constantly reinforce mutual respect; a code of conduct; and an expected standard of behavior.

30

I believe that the following rules can help to establish the foundation of discipline:

1. Establish the rules and penalties early. Enforce them regularly and discuss appending them when appropriate.

2. When you make a request and there's no immediate response, allow the benefit of the doubt and repeat yourself only to ensure that you were heard. Since new areas of behavior are always presenting themselves, it is not unreasonable to discuss why certain behavior is expected.

3. If there is still no response or if the response is slow and lazy, enforce some sort of penalty. This should ideally be something that has already been discussed.

With my son I simply say, "Mychal-David, did you hear me?" I then announce the penalty. "If you don't do what I said immediately, you will not . . ."

Disciplining our young men does not have to take the form of suspension from school or spanking at home. We can develop many forms of discipline based upon our understanding of our sons and students. We can take away privileges that he enjoys. We should develop mutual understanding in the beginning that privileges are just that! Too many of our young men receive signals at home and at school that no matter what they do, they are "entitled" to play on the basketball team, watch television, buy the latest clothes, etc.

We should establish chores at home that bear a direct relationship to the things that he wants, establishing the foundation of a "value for value" relationship, that there is value given for value received. Too many of our young men grow up believing that they are entitled to something for nothing.

4. Learn to control your tone of voice. Frequently raising your voice implies that you are not serious until you're screaming or threatening.

5. Don't discipline out of anger, discipline out of love. In your mind, you must clearly know why you're enforcing a certain discipline and you must stick to your decision. Don't confuse our young men by constantly changing your mind. You have the responsibility to display leadership and enforce your authority.

6. Don't issue idle threats! Our young men aren't buying any "wolf tickets." If you are going to discipline, then do so. If you aren't then don't threaten.

7. Don't get angry and allow yourself to speak to or threaten our young men in a disrespectful way. The foundation of discipline and mutual respect must be established early and reinforced constantly.

In my son's situation I have always issued immediate discipline when he exhibits behavior that I deem unacceptable. I always follow through immediately on any threats that I make. I demonstrate respect for his opinion and intellect by explaining, within reason, why certain behavior is expected and why certain behavior is unacceptable.

I consistently plant the seeds of greatness within my son's subconscious by telling my son that he is a Prince. He must display the highest character, integrity, and intelligence befitting one of royal heritage. I tell him that being a Prince requires him to maintain a certain standard of behavior and code of conduct. I never confront or challenge him on things that I don't feel are important enough for discipline. I never tell him not to do something or to stop doing something unless I'm prepared to discipline him if he doesn't respond immediately. And finally, I make it a point to acknowledge and reward good behavior and never to allow unacceptable behavior to go uncensored!

Every home, every school, every classroom, and every business has an unspoken code of acceptable conduct. Unfortunately, many homes and classrooms are like poorly-run businesses. Most of us have experienced going into a store where the salespeople were poorly trained, rude, lazy, uncooperative, and had a nonchalant attitude. We've also experienced businesses where the salespeople were kind, courteous, eager to help, and made us feel as though our business was really appreciated. People tend to respond in a way consistent with what they've been taught is acceptable behavior.

We, as parents and teachers, must provide the example of acceptable behavior in our homes and classrooms. Failing this, we cannot effectively communicate an acceptable code of conduct to our sons and students and more importantly to get them to buy in to this code of conduct. It is this "buy in" that establishes the foundation for teaching and for learning!

Parents and teachers who have problems with their own self-esteem and self-confidence feel that they must demonstrate to our young men who the boss is! They unwittingly are drawn into a test of will with our young men. They lose sight of the goal: to teach, discipline, love, and raise our young men. Our challenge is to create an environment of acceptable behavior without forcing our young men to lose respect and status within their peer group. Our aim is to achieve compromise without controversy.

The history of the African-American male in America is one in which we have often been stripped of our dignity, self-respect, honor, and humanity. We were brought into this country as chattel. We were not respected as human beings, but treated as property. The slave masters were not concerned with our feelings. They had no respect for our opinions. They had no compassion for our dreams and aspirations. They did everything conceivable to remove the African-American male as the head of the household and destroy our family structure.

Understanding this history, we cannot establish discipline within our young men without encouraging and rebuilding self-respect, integrity, honor, and responsibility. Our young men will respond to those who speak to them in a respectful manner; those who care enough to discuss their feelings. Here is a typical situation:

Mother: Gregory, empty the trash and clean up your room.

Gregory: I don't want to!

Mother: Don't give me any back talk.

Gregory: Why do I always have to take out the trash? And why do I have to clean up my room? No one goes in there but me anyway!

Mother: Do it because I said do it!

Many confrontations between African-American males and their parents and teachers result in the "Do it because I said do it" ultimatum. Parents and teachers find it easier to issue ultimatums than to discuss and explain the reasons why certain responsibilities are given to their sons or students. Displaying this type of dictatorship attitude will not empower our young men to make their own decisions in life. In fact, constantly challenging and threatening them often results in their conscious efforts to disobey!

I'm not suggesting that all of our decisions should be subjected to discussion and debate prior to our sons or students obeying our instructions. I'm suggesting that we can become better parents and teachers by thinking through why we want our young men to display a certain standard of behavior and to assume certain types of responsibilities.

For example:

Mother: Gregory, empty the trash and clean up your room.

Gregory: I don't want to!

Mother: Gregory, part of your responsibilities in this household is to empty the trash and to keep your room clean. Why would you want to have trash in the house? You know that it attracts bugs and bacteria. And you know that you're supposed to clean your room every day. One day when you're rich and famous you can hire a maid to clean your room and a butler to empty your trash. However, today, that's part of your responsibilities.

Gregory: Why do I always have to take out the trash? And why do I have to clean up my room? No one goes in there but me anyway!

Mother: Gregory, you know that we all have certain responsibilities. I have responsibilities to go to work where people depend on me. I have to prepare dinner daily, plan the family budget, do the laundry, and pay an assortment of monthly bills so that the electricity, gas, and telephone aren't disconnected. And it doesn't matter if we don't have any guests all week. Whenever someone does come to visit our home, I want to have pride in our home just like I have pride in you. Now, let's not waste any more time complaining. No one has to remind me to pay the bills, or prepare dinner. So why should I have to remind you of your responsibilities?

This approach is not as quick and easy as simply saying, "Do it because I said do it!" This does, however, replace dictatorship with teaching. It discusses responsibilities and provides leadership examples. It explains why accepting responsibility is important and why these particular responsibilities have been established. It plants the seed that Gregory will become successful and that he will be capable of hiring maids and butlers. It discusses pride in one's self and one's home. And it concludes with the example that complaining is not desirable behavior. It also empowers Gregory for a peer group encounter:

Peer: Why does your mother make you take out the trash? I don't have to do anything at home. I never have to clean up my room.

Gregory: Well, at my house everyone has responsibilities. My mother goes to work, cooks dinner and pays all the bills. So I guess taking out the trash and cleaning up my room is not too much to ask. And besides, it makes her happy to have a clean house, you never know who will drop by.

Never speak to our young men in negative terms when censoring their behavior. When John doesn't do his homework it's more encouraging to tell him that you know that he is brilliant, that he is capable of extraordinary things, and that the homework is meant to help him in developing the strong foundation that he will need to achieve his goals in life. Rather than "John, not again, why don't you ever do your homework, if you don't do your homework you're going to get an F!" When Wayne is clowning in class it is more encouraging to bring Wayne into the discussion by asking him to comment on the topic of discussion or to discuss how the topic is relative to his life, rather than to tell him "Wayne, shut-up or I'll send you to the Principal's office." We'll often find that our most disruptive students have extraordinary leadership skills. Our challenge is to properly focus those skills and channel those energies into a tremendously powerful force within our classrooms, schools, and communities.

If we can get our young men to decide upon an acceptable code of conduct, we can use positive peer pressure in reinforcing this code of conduct. This will make our jobs easier and provide a foundation for reinforcing desirable behavior in our schools and classrooms. A clear code of conduct should be adopted by the school and developed for each classroom beginning the first day of the school year.

EXERCISE #5

1. Write down your classroom or home Code of Conduct. Develop these through discussions with your young men. Decide upon and mutually buy into appropriate forms of discipline. Post the Code of Conduct, together with the agreed upon discipline, on a bulletin board or refrigerator or in some other place where it can be referred to. You will discover peer pressure working for you to enforce the conduct that the class has determined appropriate. Mutual respect is developed as a result of your commitment to enforce what the class has accepted.

2. Incorporate into your teaching, and/or parenting style, firm, yet loving ways to communicate desired behavior. Never allow deviations from the code of conduct to go unnoticed. This may mean simply walking around the room and placing your hand on someone's shoulder without allowing them to interrupt the lesson.

3. Avoid confronting our young men unless you're prepared to enforce your authority. Be careful not to make them lose face among their peers, always allow them the opportunity to retain their dignity and the respect of their peer group.

4. Here is a list of things to discuss in your classroom and/or home:
   - An acceptable dress code
   - Acceptable posture
   - Acceptable personal hygiene
   - Appropriate speech
   - Appropriate manners
   - An appropriate hand shake

- Pride
- Dignity
- Integrity
- Character
- Kindness
- Love for self
- Love for each other
- Our relationship to the world community
- Achieving respect without violence
- Leading by example
- Respect for self and others
- Social problems and solutions

Discuss these ideas and issues within the context of the philosophical writings and teachings of African-American men whom our young men respect and admire (e.g., Malcolm X, Martin Luther King, Jr., etc.). In this way we help them to develop and articulate their own philosophies.

5. Expand this list to incorporate the unique problems and situations in your school or home. As you develop, discuss, and identify the acceptable behavior in your classroom and/or home, do so with the focus on the young men achieving their goals.

6. Demonstrate to them that there is a correlation:

    - Between their behavior and goal achievement.
    - Between their behavior and social advancement.
    - Between their behavior and success in their lives.

7. Build the foundation of acceptable behavior upon the cornerstone of pride in themselves, responsibility to their community; their family, future children, future wife; and of their developing a personal quest for excellence. Laughing, giggling, negative words, and any other signs of discouragement must not be tolerated. Work toward bonding with our young men and help them to bond with each other.

8. Discuss their ideas and help them to formulate their opinions about personal responsibilities. Talk about how African-American men are portrayed in the media and what obstacles confront them in education and careers. Discuss how their attitude and character will affect how they respond to the challenges and obstacles confronting them.

OUR CODE OF CONDUCT

1. We will begin each day by affirming our individual and collective greatness.

2. We will begin each day by giving each other a hug (or handshake).

3. We will always do our best to help each other achieve their goals and dreams.

4. We will always strive for the highest character, integrity, and honesty.

5. We will always maintain a passion for excellence in what we do. Anything worth doing is worth doing well!

6. We will always maintain the manners and posture worthy of a royal heritage, carrying ourselves with pride and dignity.

7. We will always demonstrate respect for ourselves and for the rights and property of others.

8. We will never say negative or discouraging things to each other.

9. We will never hit, bite, kick or scream at each other.

10. We will apply each of the first nine codes of conduct as though someone was always watching.

If a man is called to be a streetsweeper, he should sweep streets even as Michelangelo painted, or Beethoven composed music, or Shakespeare wrote poetry. He should sweep streets so well that all the hosts of heaven and earth will pause to say, here lived a great streetsweeper who did his job well.

– Martin Luther King, Jr.

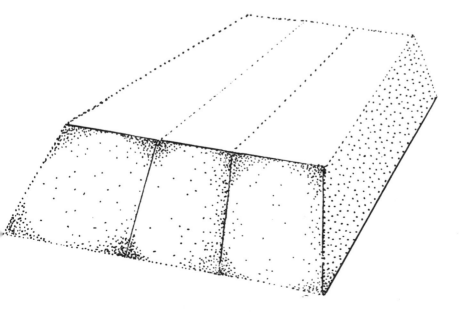

Block 3

PERSONAL RESPONSIBILITY

Jawanza Kunjufu, in *Countering the Conspiracy to Destroy Black Boys, Volume II,* discusses the idea of mothers who raise their daughters and love their sons. He discusses how mothers give their daughters a multitude of responsibilities, while absolving their sons of all but the basic household chores. In my workshops, this is always a highly debated area of discussion. Although many parents and teachers agree with this idea there are many mothers who view this as a personal attack on their ability to raise their sons. Some of their comments are:

"It's a man's responsibility to give my son responsibilities."

"I do the best that I can with my son, but he's so strong willed."

"Boys will be boys."

I have also seen teachers assign classroom responsibilities to their female students while allowing our "boys to be boys."

One cold winter night in Chicago my friend Jerry and I gathered all of the paper and wood that we could find around the apartment complex that we lived in. We found a nice cozy place under a back porch and dumped all of the paper and wood into a trash can and started a fire. We didn't start the fire to keep warm, we just wanted to see how big a fire we could burn! Fortunately, the janitor of the building came by and put the fire out before we could burn down the building. He grabbed both of us by the collar and took us home. All during the time that my mother was whipping my butt she kept screaming at me, "Why did you set the fire, why did you set the fire?" She kept whipping me and asking why I set the fire and I kept crying and saying, "I don't know."

Finally, with her arms tired and out of breath, my mother grabbed me and started shaking me saying, "Jerry started the fire, didn't he?" As if on cue, I started nodding my head and saying, "Yes ma'am Jerry did it, he sure did, I didn't do nothing."

My mother, like so many other mothers, didn't want to believe that her son was behaving irresponsibly and had nearly burned down the building. Many of our young men stroll through our homes, schools, and communities refusing to accept responsibility for themselves and their actions. Many of our parents after receiving telephone calls from schools or the police about trouble that their sons have been involved in immediately defend their sons and their actions. They refuse to believe that their sons are capable of such behavior. I've heard mothers excuse the actions of our young men by blaming their peers for influencing their behavior or on their financial circumstances or on their communities.

Our young men don't benefit from our excusing irresponsible, ill-mannered, and disrespectful behavior. It is our responsibility as parents, educators, and concerned citizens to teach our young men responsibilities and to hold them accountable for their actions. To prepare our boys to become men we must not only demand that they accept responsibilities, but that they accept them fully. We must demand that they not only do their jobs and perform their chores but that they do them well.

We've already identified that many of our young men who come from single-parent, female-headed households, lack positive male role models, and come from communities whose residents feel powerless to change their situations. Our young men are refusing to accept responsibility for themselves and their actions. Parents are failing to accept responsibility for developing effective parenting strategies. Teachers are failing to accept responsibility for developing effective lesson plans and teaching strategies. Government, civic, education, and community leaders are failing to accept responsibility and failing to work together in developing effective strategies to resolve the problems and issues within our schools and communities. Our young men are simply following the example of those who are failing them.

We are not helping our young men when parents feel a sense of accomplishment by simply getting them out of the house to go to school! Or, when teachers feel a sense of accomplishment by simply getting our young men to sit still in class! Our young men must be given clear responsibilities and held accountable for getting up on time, getting properly dressed, and being properly groomed. They must be held responsible for fulfilling household duties (e.g., making the bed, cleaning up after eating, cleaning up the bathroom, etc.) before going to school and that after school, homework comes before basketball. The foundation and acceptance of responsibility must begin at home and be reinforced in school and throughout the community. It is never too early to begin building the foundation of responsibility and self-respect. We get so excited when babies take their first steps, speak their first words, and become potty trained. Why then do we allow our young men (after taking those first steps) to walk around with their pants falling off, dragging their feet, with that lazy and shiftless look? Why do we allow our young men to mumble and speak expressing no self-confidence and self-assurance in their voices? After all of our efforts to potty train our baby boys, why do we allow our young men to leave our bathrooms as though a daily cyclone blows through our homes?

Many of our young men in gangs and prison have never had a discussion with their parents about their responsibilities to themselves, their families, their communities and their relationships with other human beings. The gang violence that

47

I've witnessed in Los Angeles, and while growing up in Chicago, is not being committed by young men who have lost respect for human life, but by young men who have never been taught respect for human life.

When our young men come from homes where personal responsibilities are not being taught, we cannot allow ourselves the luxury of believing that it's simply somebody else's problem. This has become America's problem. We have a human responsibility to stop shaking our heads and to open our mouths. Through kindness, love, and compassion we must discuss with the young men in our schools, churches, businesses, and communities the concepts that will help them understand how to live respectful, fulfilling, successful lives. We must provide leadership and counseling before they father babies, drop out of school, join gangs, commit crimes, and go to prisons.

Helping our young men to assume personal responsibilities builds self-esteem. It prepares our young men for the future. It gives them pride and self-respect.

Ron Weaver, in *Beyond Identity: Education and the Future Role of Black Americans*, points out: "Several properties of classroom organization have been identified as important for development of a high degree of self-esteem in children. First, the children, especially minority children, must be afforded a sense of mastery — the degree to which they view themselves as able to manipulate events and achieve desired goals — over what happens to them in school. Through such mastery or decision-making opportunity, children may develop self-responsibility. This, in turn, may provide motivation in the sense that the children feel they, rather than someone else, are responsible for their success and failure. Subsequently, this role of self-direction may provide greater initiative in seeking success in school since Black children's views of the environment of the school — how open and manipulable the environment seems to be — has been noted as more important to Black children than their competence in determining success."

George Henderson, in the same book, points out: "Studies in the foundations of humanistic education for Black students also indicate that Black students are better served when they have an active voice in the decision-making process which attends learning and accept the responsibility of the consummation of the decisions made. Indeed, self-concept and personal esteem are heightened when students share in their own educational development and emotional growth." We can expand upon this strategy by giving our young men rotating responsibilities in the classroom:

- Collect homework.
- Quote for the day.
- Explain how they've put into action the codes of conduct in their lives.
- Attendance taker.
- Responsible for closing the door when the bell rings.
- Each day assign a different young man the responsibility of reciting a moment in African-American history.
- Have students give each other oral quizzes.
- Have groups quiz each other.

Good managers and supervisors understand the importance of effectively delegating responsibilities. This is how employees are prepared for growth and advancement. A teacher who effectively delegates responsibilities to our young men not only makes their job of teaching easier, but prepares our young men for assuming personal responsibilities in their lives and business responsibilities in their future employment. Parents must establish personal responsibilities early in our young men. They must be held responsible for keeping their rooms clean and picking up after themselves. They must have regular duties in the same manner as everyone else in the household. We must raise our sons to become the type of men that we would want our daughters to marry and our community to respect!

We must establish and maintain regular dialogue with our young men in all areas of responsibility (e.g., sex, drugs, religion, gangs, pregnancy, destruction of property, etc.). Although religion, prayer, and worship of God is not taught in our public schools, parents must assume the responsibility of helping our young men to develop a solid religious foundation. Our young men cannot be sufficiently empowered to deal with the complexities of the problems confronting African-American men without a solid religious foundation. The life-saving decisions that they must make in their lives (e.g., drugs, gangs, teenage pregnancy, etc.) must be guided spiritually and morally. Our schools, businesses, churches, and the community at-large must assume a leadership role and provide clear examples of accepting responsibility for ourselves.

Professional organizations whose members have roots within our communities (e.g., National Medical Association, National Dental Association, National Bar Association, National Association of Black MBAs, National Urban Bankers, sororities, fraternities, etc.) must step forward to contribute more time, money, and creativity to demonstrate leadership in accepting the responsibility to resolve the problems and issues confronting our community.

There are many African-American professionals, particularly our athletes and entertainers, who live in multi-room, multi-million dollar mansions who have the power and resources to give our young men who spend day after day in orphanages and other state agencies the experience of a life-time by opening their homes to these young men. There are other young men from poor families who are top students and role models in their schools who are losing their lives to street violence because they don't have the financial resources to enroll in a safer school.

Our doctors, lawyers, bankers, and business management professionals who have reached the pinnacle of their respective careers have the time and resources to establish community health care programs, small business training, start-up capital, legal services, personal skills training and development. This provides leadership in developing solutions, and the example that we are willing to accept responsibility for our community.

Most corporations provide matching grant programs where the company will contribute an amount equal to the employee's contribution to non-profit organizations. We must accept the responsibility to seek out such programs and direct these corporate resources into programs and organizations that are working within our communities.

I participate at hundreds of professional meetings throughout the country and I am amazed at the large numbers of professionals with roots within our communities who have never participated in a Career Day program and have had no involvement in community, or volunteer programs which directly impact upon the future of our community. As Patricia Russell-McCloud, a nationally renowned African-American professional speaker has said in her keynote presentations before our business and professional organizations, "If not you, who? If not now, when?"

By getting more African-American men involved in leading discussions in our classrooms our teachers can build upon and integrate those social and moral issues into their classroom discussions about history, social sciences, economics, etc.

Discussions could evolve from such questions as:

- What are some of the things that we must think about before having children? (E.g., health care, day care, food, clothes, education, where we'll live, where we'll work, etc.)
- What are the physical changes that the body undergoes as a result of drugs? What are Crack Babies?

- What is the history of gangs? When were the first gangs organized?

- How did religion evolve in ancient Africa? What did it have in common with the religions of today?

- If you were to drop out of school today how would you prepare for your retirement? How much money will you need to live on?

- How many young Black men die annually from homicides and violent crime? How does this relate to the number killed during the Vietnam war? How could these confrontations have been resolved without violence?

- Why should we be responsible for voting?

- Why should we serve jury duty?

Combine these with other questions to provide the catalyst for classroom discussions about the broad range of responsibilities that our young men must assume. Help our young men develop the thinking and reasoning skills needed to make life-saving decisions. Parents should engage in regular discussions with their sons about "why" they should be responsible for certain things. Discuss with them what types of responsibilities they must assume to become the head of a household (e.g., budget planning, professional employment, running a business, running a household, etc.).

Our young men must be taught how to develop philosophies of living; the personal rules that we apply to how we live our lives; how we deal with problems and conflicts in our lives. The concepts of diligence, determination, perseverance, fortitude, integrity, and accepting responsibility for one's actions must be regularly discussed in our homes. Much of what our young men see in the movies and read in magazines glamorize criminals, drugs, and alcohol abuse. Our young men are constantly being exposed to movies which promote violence as the solution to resolving interpersonal conflicts. Our young men are further guided by the example of immoral and unethical people cruising the neighborhoods of America in expensive cars making their wealth by selling death. Too many of our young men believe that this is the only way to make it. We are not spending enough time convincing them that the possibilities and the opportunities are endless; that success and self-respect can indeed go hand in hand.

BONUS EXERCISE

Discuss the following poem with your students or son. Ask them to describe how the poem relates to their experiences.

A Man Is . . .

A man is not quick to anger
>He's not one whose quick to brawl

If you see a man bullying others
>He's not a man at all

A man is not a quitter
>He's not one to turn and run

When the going gets rough, he gets tough
>He'll remain 'til the job is done

A man takes no satisfaction
>in seeing another fail

He encourages all to try
>and to believe that they can prevail

A man will never boast or brag
>or kick sand in your eye

He'll stand firm on his conviction
>with his head held to the sky

A man will always lend a hand
>when he finds a friend in need

His character and his integrity
>makes him a true friend indeed

© Mychal Wynn

When you control a man's thinking you do not have to worry about his actions. You do not have to tell him not to stand here or go yonder. He will find his 'proper place' and will stay in it. You do not need to send him to the back door. He will go without being told. In fact, if there is no back door, he will cut one for his special benefit.

— Carter G. Woodson

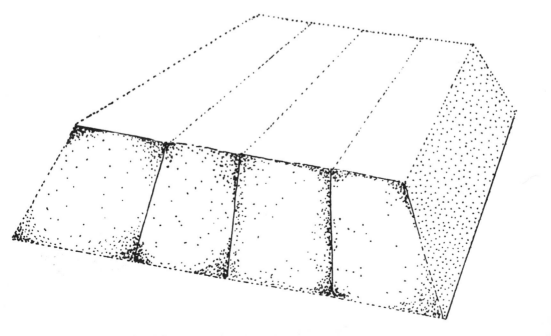

We must inspire to aspire

Block 4

TEACHER/PARENT EXPECTATIONS

Our young men, like most people, aspire toward what they know others have done. Their views and ideas of their potential will largely reflect the success achieved by their friends, family, and others within their community. Their vision of success will be limited, or enhanced, by those around them. Our young men aspire to become athletes and entertainers because they believe these to be fields accessible to them. They see professional basketball teams starting all Black players and they see the entertainment superstars with material wealth.

They don't see many Black doctors, lawyers, and other professionals portrayed on television or in the community. Even when they say that they want to become doctors, lawyers, or educators, they don't say it with conviction. They never speak in terms of becoming a "great doctor," or a "renowned attorney," or a "legendary educator!" Our young men are not aspiring to become outstanding doctors, lawyers, businessmen, and educators, because we are not inspiring them to do so!

Teacher/Parent Expectations represents the single most important building block in our young men seeking an education that prepares them to achieve excellence and empowers them to develop solutions to the many conflicts confronting them in their lives. This is the cornerstone of our pyramid.

Janice Hale-Benson, in *Black Children: Their Roots, Culture, and Learning Styles,* states: "We know that the system is not working because of the disproportionate number of Black children who are labeled mentally retarded and placed in special classes. We know that the system is not working because of the disproportionate number of Black children who are being suspended, expelled, and pushed out of schools."

Roy Weaver, in *Beyond Identity: Education and the Future Role of Black Americans,* points out that "Since Black children are often viewed by their teachers as incapable of success, they tend to perform at low levels and internalize negative feelings. For Black children, as is the case with other minority children usually possessing values differing from those of their teachers, little of what the teachers say or the attitudes instilled are considered related to their life outside the school."

The idea of the aspirations of our young men being linked to our expectations is further reinforced by Carter G. Woodson who points out: "What Negroes are now being taught does not bring their minds into harmony with life as they must face it. When a Negro student works his way through college by polishing shoes he does not think of making a special study of the science underlying the production and distribution of leather and its products that he may some day figure in this sphere. The Negro boy sent to college by a mechanic seldom dreams of learning mechanical engineering to build upon the foundation his father had laid, that in years to come he may figure as a contractor or consulting engineer."

We must raise our expectations of our young men to greater levels of achievement in all the areas that we have previously discussed. We must consistently communicate our expectations of excellence; that we not only believe that they are capable, but that we expect them to excel. We must establish and reinforce their personal responsibilities, character, and behavior in a manner consistent with our expectations of exceptional goal achievement. We must begin to look at, speak to, and encourage our young men in a way that communicates that we believe that they are capable of owning businesses and rebuilding their communities; that we expect them to take responsibility for, and ownership of, their lives and their communities.

Our classrooms, schools, homes, and communities should consciously affirm that our young men are capable of not only striving for excellence but of achieving excellence. When a young man sets a goal to play in the National Basketball Association (NBA) or to teach or practice law, we must communicate in everything that we say and do: "You have the power to do that!"

"You have the power to not only play in the NBA but to own an NBA franchise. You have the power to become a coach or general manager. You have the power to become NBA commissioner."

"You have the power to not only practice law, but to become the greatest lawyer the world has ever known. You have the power to become a partner in a multi-million dollar law firm. You have the power to become a Supreme Court justice. You have the power to challenge the United States Constitution to ensure the end of inequality and injustice in our judicial system."

"You have the power to not only teach but to become a great educator. You have the power to become an expert in education. You have the power to become a teacher of teachers. You have the power to become a university president, superintendent of schools, or president of the school board."

We can't simply tell our young men to get a good education, get a good job, and work hard. Their response is, "Get a job for what; work hard for whom?" We must raise our expectations. Every young man must be encouraged to believe that he has the power to become the next great scientist, attorney, astronaut, educator, musician, historian, or whatever he aspires to become. They must be encouraged to believe that:

Their attitude will determine their altitude.

They are limited only by the scope of their dreams.

Our young men will raise their achievement level if they believe that we believe in them. They will gain confidence in themselves if they believe that we have confidence in them. They will begin to reach for the stars if they believe that we will help them to get there.

EXERCISE #6

1. At the beginning of the school year, outline for your young men what you intend to accomplish.

2. Engage in a discussion about their dreams, their future, the current situation of African-Americans, and what you intend to do to assist them in achieving their goals. After helping to identify their goals you are going to make a commitment to ensure that they have every opportunity to achieve those goals. Whether or not they achieve their goals will depend entirely upon whether or not they have the commitment and determination to achieve them. Whether or not they have the courage and fortitude not to quit!

As the leader, it is your single most important purpose to ensure that they have every opportunity to succeed. You must do everything in your power to give them the information that they need to achieve their goals. They simply have the responsibility to learn.

Example:

"As your teacher/parent, I am here for the single purpose of helping you to achieve your goals. I am committed to helping to give you every possible chance to make your dreams come true. All of the things that we study will in some way become an important part of the things that you will need to know to make your dreams come true. Whatever you want to become, we will work together to see that you get there. Whether you want to become a professional athlete, a doctor, a lawyer, a teacher, a musician, a chemist, a mathematician, a physicist, an entrepreneur, a journalist, or a movie star, I am here to help you to become whatever you really want to be. I guarantee that by the end of the school year, you will have developed some of the important skills, knowledge, talents, and understanding that you will need to become the greatest at what you want to do. This classroom is going to become supercharged with your dreams.

We are going to help each other, love each other, and encourage each other to become the best that we possibly can and to achieve whatever we want to achieve in our lives."

Encourage them to set goals; not just ordinary goals but extraordinary goals! You are going to make a commitment to ensure that they have every opportunity to achieve their goals, encouraging them always to develop a commitment to themselves and their dreams; to run the race until they cross the finish line. A commitment that says, "If I don't finish first this time, I am going to practice and run the race again." Make it clear that they will be held personally responsible for their actions, their attitude, their homework, and their respect for others. On these issues there can be no comprise!

EXERCISE #7

1. At the beginning of the school year, have your young
    men take a sheet of paper and draw a frame around it
    so that the sheet of paper represents a mirror. Have
    them write inside the mirror how they see themselves.

2. Do the same thing for yourself.

    Example:

    "In my mirror I see an attractive man who has a brilliant mind,
    who is capable of achieving anything that he sets his mind to.
    I see a man who is a strong father, loyal, faithful, and loving
    husband. I see a man who believes that he can stand upon the
    word of God. I see a man who is a trusted, loyal, and com-
    mitted friend. I see a man whose parents, friends, and rela-
    tives admire and respect him. I see a man who always
    encourages others to believe that they have the potential and
    the power to overcome obstacles and fulfill their dreams. I
    see a man capable of becoming one of the world's greatest
    authors and public speakers, helping people to realize the
    greatness within themselves."

3. Take the papers and write on them how you see the in-
    dividual. Say such things as: "I see you becoming the
    greatest speaker that the world has ever known" or "I
    see you as a Prince with a lineage stretching back to
    the Kings of Africa" or "I see you as a great poet and
    philosopher."

    This simple exercise will help you to see the potential in our
    young men and help them to see the greatness in themselves!

4. Make copies of the papers with your comments for your
    file and return the originals. Repeat this exercise at the
    end of the school year.

Our young men have a history of excellence when they're expected to excel. We witness this in competitive athletics, in oratorical contests, in music, art and numerous other endeavors in which they have an interest and receive encouragement.

Our young men have not only become some of the greatest athletes in the history of mankind, they have become some of the greatest orators, inventors, soldiers, human rights activists, professionals, entrepreneurs, educators, mathematicians, physicists, doctors, political and social leaders, novelists, poets, and artists. In every field of endeavor, our young men have proved themselves capable when given the opportunity and encouragement to succeed.

Expectations of our young men should reflect our achievements in establishing the foundation of civilization in Africa, not limited to perceptions based upon the media projections of the crisis in the black family, nor of the gangs, drugs, crime, and violence associated with our young men on the nightly newscasts.

Our young men must be taught that they have a rich past in which their forefathers were the first doctors, philosophers, mathematicians, and scholars; that the mothers of their race were queens of such mesmerizing beauty that kings and emperors throughout the world were hypnotized and captivated by them.

Our expectations should communicate to our young men that we not only expect them to strive for excellence, but that we believe that they are capable of achieving excellence. Empowering our young men means communicating in every way, in everything that we do, that they are capable of extraordinary things; that we appreciate the ordinary things that are done, but that we believe they are capable of more; that they have the potential for greatness and to become the best at whatever they want to do; and that they have the power to achieve anything that they want to achieve.

America has lost its position as the world leader in industry, technology, and education because we've lost pride in the work we do. Many of us feel powerless to change our situations so we accept mediocrity and a life of defeat, hopelessness, and failure. Teachers feel powerless because they can't control school administration or the student's home environment. Parents feel powerless because they no longer believe that they're capable of moving to a new community, a new house, or getting a better job. Our community feels powerless to keep our young men out of gangs, off drugs, and safe from the violent crime surrounding them.

Because we are feeling powerless about our lives, we transfer those feelings on to our young men. We can't help our young men to see a better, brighter, prosperous future for themselves unless we can see it in them. We can't convince them to pursue excellence unless we strive for excellence in our own lives.

We must begin to see in our young men the potential of the oratory and resilience of Dr. Martin Luther King, Jr.; the brilliance of Dr. Charles Drew and Dr. George Washington Carver; the courage and conviction of Paul Robeson; and the business savvy of John Johnson. Our attitudes toward our young men, and our expectations for their capability for achievement should bring to life the words of the poem "Be A Winner."

Be A Winner

If all around you are quitting, as they sometimes do
If your critics are many and friends are few
If obstacles confront you at every turn
Remember the lessons that Winners learned . . .

To stop and quit you will never win
Until you decide to try it again
When life's little hurdles slow you down
Just steady your pace and hold your ground

Hold fast to your dreams, as they can come true
When you do the best that you can possibly do
To win you must believe that you will not fail
Perseverance is the breeze that fills your sail

Although the unexpected may rock your boat
Winners will weather the storm remaining afloat
Conceive it, believe it, and know that you can
Continue step by step according to plan

Stand up and be counted so that the world will see
That you believe in becoming the best you can be
Accept the challenges of life and you'll continue to find
That winning is the spirit of living
. . . it's merely a state of mind

© *Mychal Wynn*

If there is no struggle, there is no progress. Those who profess to favor freedom, and yet deprecate agitation, are men who want crops without plowing up the ground. They want rain without thunder and lightning. They want the ocean without the awful roar of its many waters. This struggle may be a moral one; or it may be a physical one; or it may be both moral and physical; but it must be a struggle. Power concedes nothing without demand.

— Frederick Douglass

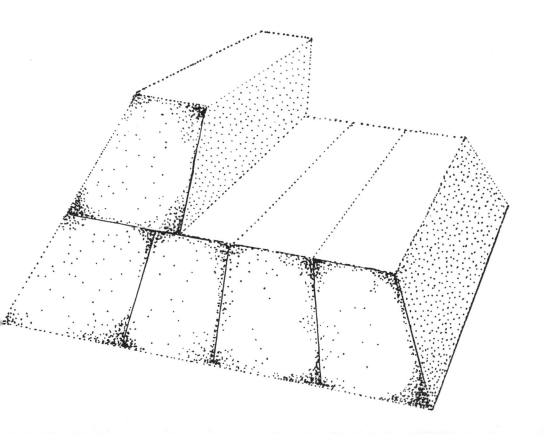

Block 5

FOCUS/IDENTIFY GOALS

In laying the blocks of our foundation, we have identified some of the elements that influence how our young men establish goals: their environments, their peer groups, their self-confidence, their self-esteem, their understanding of their history, their belief in their future, and their spiritual foundation all influence goal setting.

The scope and magnitude of a person's goals is rooted in their experience, self-confidence, and faith. When one has experienced the thrill of victory, the satisfaction and adulation of extraordinary achievement, or the praise and acknowledgment that accompany's winning, one has an undeniable advantage over those who have never had such experience. Setting and achieving smaller goals gives a person confidence in their ability to set and to achieve larger goals.

Some of our young men are innately self-confident and assertive. They are born with the "attitude" for achievement. Others develop their confidence and receive their assurance through our loving, nurturing, and encouragement. In either case we must help our young men develop spiritual awareness and enlightenment. A spiritual foundation and deeply-rooted belief that they are capable of overcoming obstacles through a higher source will help them to establish goals and remain confident in their ability to succeed despite the obstacles and challenges that confront them.

People who feel and believe in this way, have become empowered to attain extraordinary levels of achievement and generally set extraordinary, aggressive goals for themselves. Unfortunately, most of our young men don't fall into this category. Most of our young men begin school eager to learn, to explore, and to achieve. However, by the fourth grade, in what has been widely studied and labeled the "Fourth Grade Syndrome," in large numbers they lose their motivation, self-confidence, self-esteem, and desire to pursue extraordinary levels of achievement. I would highly recommend that you examine the issues leading up to this phenomenon. Janice Hale-Benson and Jawanza Kunjufu have examined the Fourth Grade Syndrome in their respective books (listed as references in the back of this book).

Many of our young men have never experienced winning. The emotional uplifting of having people pat you on the back and congratulate you on being the best. The personal sense of joy and fulfillment of having set a goal and achieved it. They don't have a family tradition of extraordinary achievement. They may live in communities where people don't feel empowered to control their situations and define their futures. It is by successfully laying the previous blocks of our pyramid that we have begun to establish for them a new foundation and to define for them new possibilities. We must take them as they are with whatever dreams they have and help them to experience daily success in the things that they enjoy. We can take their ordinary goals and redefine them in extraordinary terms.

During workshops I am often asked: "How do you motivate these young men?" Our young men have all been motivated at one time or another by one thing or another. They were motivated in preschool and kindergarten. They were excited about going to school. Many of them talked about their kindergarten teachers all the time, "Ms. Smith this, Ms. Smith that, Ms. Smith says so and so, or Ms. Smith told me such and such." Our challenge is to discover what motivates them today!

Many are motivated to obtain the latest clothes, to play in the NBA, to memorize and develop rap music, to be popular within their peer groups, etc. In interviews with our athletes many say that they were motivated to buy their mothers a house or to create new opportunities for their families. Walk into any of our classrooms and offer "free" tickets to a basketball game or a concert, a free shopping spree, or a pair of sneakers of their choice and see how motivated our young men are! We need to bring that which motivates them into the classroom and make that a part of our curriculum.

Many teachers don't even attempt to motivate our young men. They further communicate through lowered expectations that our young men don't have the ability or capacity, to achieve extraordinary things. Useni Eugene Perkins, in *Harvesting New Generations: The Positive Development of Black Youth*, quotes from Booker T. Washington: "The world should not pass judgment upon the Negro, and especially upon the Negro youth, too quickly or too harshly. The Negro boy has obstacles, discouragements, and temptations to battle with that are little known to those not situated as he is. When a white boy undertakes a task, it is taken for granted that he will succeed. On the other hand, people are usually surprised if the Negro boy does not fail. In a word, the Negro youth starts out with the presumption against him."

With the deck already stacked against our young men we cannot allow anyone to discourage them from setting extraordinary goals for themselves. Have we forgotten how many in our community are first generation college graduates? Our mothers and fathers constantly encouraged us to do what they did not have the opportunity to do. Have we forgotten that many people thought that we were incapable of college-level study; that we were strong but could never become studious; that we could plow the land but that we could never own the land?

When our young men become bored and disinterested in what the teacher is teaching, we simply assume that the fault lies within our young men and not with the method of teaching. When we establish high expectations, and constantly encourage our young men toward the highest levels of achievement, we will see our young men establishing higher goals for themselves.

One of the common questions that I'm asked at workshops is: "Aren't we setting our young men up for failure when we establish goals that they can't possibly achieve?" Anyone who would ask that question doesn't understand that African-Americans, despite all of our problems and the apparently insurmountable obstacles confronting us, have proved to be people of extraordinary resilience. Any student of history knows that we have endured terrible hardships. Our young men who begin life with the deck stacked against them have never surrendered.

Our men studied and taught themselves to read when it was forbidden and life threatening to do so. Our men stood and spoke out against the treatment of African-Americans when they were surely signing their death warrants to do so.

Have we forgotten that the Slave Masters believed that life for Blacks outside of slavery would be impossible?

Have we forgotten that behavioral scientists were quite convinced that the Negro mind was limited genetically in the scope of its comprehension?

Have we forgotten that there was a time when it was unthinkable that a Black man could build a multi-million dollar business, become a Doctor; break the chains of slavery; or make a serious challenge for the Presidency of the United States of America?

My response is always: "After enduring what we've endured in this society, there are no goals that are unachievable!" Who are we to determine which of our young men is capable of extraordinary achievement? How dare we establish goals that are limited in scope because we don't believe that our young men are capable!

Don't worry about setting our young men up for failure; set them up for success! Establish and affirm for them extraordinary goals. However, before you can persuade them to believe in themselves, you must first believe in them.

EXERCISE #8

1. Have men (teachers, coaches, principal, custodians, etc.) involved at your school make regular visits to the classroom or home.

2. Have them talk about setting goals and the concepts of diligence, determination, integrity, perseverance, passion for excellence, inner strength, and character that are needed to achieve those goals.

3. Have them encourage our young men to develop strong handshakes, to speak clearly, to introduce themselves with confidence, to hold their heads up, to walk with a strong posture, and to say their names with pride. Help them to develop the character that accompany's being a winner.

4. Have local African-American businessmen, professionals, police and firemen, plumbers, electricians, etc., visit your classroom or home on a regular basis.

5. Many professionals can arrange for a few hours on a regular basis to "Adopt-A-School." If there are enough African-American men in your school, have them "Adopt-A-Student."

They can visit different classrooms each week so that our young men can see, touch, and hear men with whom they can identify; men who believe in them. Eventually this "bonding" can carry over into the hallways of the school and onto the streets of the community. Our young men will begin to see men who care. Men who have not only helped them to establish goals but men who will continue to encourage them toward achieving their goals.

EXERCISE #9

1. If you performed the previous exercise where you had your young men write down goals, list every goal on a sheet of paper to be distributed or posted.

    Write the list so that it reads:

    - Malcolm Robinson is going to become a great educator.
    - Robert Smith is going to become a great basketball player and businessman.
    - Muhammad Akbar is going to become a great physicist.

2. Have your young men develop a list of fantasy goals, e.g., to become President, a billionaire, to own a million dollar home, etc. Encourage them to dream of their highest and most outrageous fantasies.

3. Repeat step one.

4. Select several of the goals from each list and have a discussion identifying the things needed and steps to be taken to achieve the goals on each list. Write down and develop the list of ideas for as long as time permits. Discuss the amount of work, study, diligence and determination required for performing each step.

This discussion should be performed periodically throughout the year. It will help to change the attitudes about their ability to achieve their goals. It will also demonstrate that even goals considered outrageous are achievable when we can identify the steps required in achieving them. Each time this exercise is performed, our young men are encouraged to look for solutions to their problems and are being taught how to identify the necessary steps to achieving their goals. It will teach them that their dreams are achievable. Over time the goals defined by our young men will expand and grow in magnitude. Their expectations will grow as will our own. They are becoming empowered!

Michael Jordan, one of the most extraordinary basketball players in the history of the National Basketball Association, is idolized by hundreds of thousands of our young men. He is one of the most highly-respected athletes ever. When I visit schools and ask our young men what their goals are, countless numbers of them immediately respond, "I want to become a basketball player like Michael Jordan." This response is made despite statistics which indicate that:

- 1,000,000 boys dreamed of playing in the NBA.
- 400,000 made the high school team.
- 4,000 made the college team.
- 35 made an NBA team.
- 7 started.
- 4 years was the average career length.

These young men have established a goal for themselves. They can be seen playing basketball on snow-covered playgrounds. They know all the NBA statistics. They can be found cutting classes to spend the entire day in the gymnasium. These young men have developed a passion for what they believe to be their way to a brighter future. They believe that basketball is the "ticket" to a better life. These young men don't care about the statistics, and they don't want to hear "What if you don't make it!"

The situation I have just described is referred to as the "Michael Jordan Phenomena." Simply stated, it exists when our young men aspire to become professional athletes. In understanding the Michael Jordan Phenomena we must accept that this is their dream; this is where their passion lies.

Perhaps they are like me. My father wasn't a scholar. He wasn't a professional. He didn't aspire to read books on history, philosophy, or religion. What he and I shared was sports. We followed the Chicago Bulls, the Bears, the White Sox and the Cubs. We didn't sit around discussing philosophy or history but we knew the batting averages, scoring, and rebounding leaders. We watched Saturday Night Boxing and made friendly wagers on the boxers.

So if a young man aspires to be the second coming of Michael Jordan, don't discourage him. If you do, he won't sit still in your classroom, he won't do his homework because in his mind there is no relationship between what you're teaching and what he needs to know to make it into the NBA. He will take the easiest classes so that he can maintain the minimum grade point average necessary to stay on the team.

EXERCISE #10

Willie wants to become the next Michael Jordan. He wears Air Jordan sneakers and Chicago Bulls warm-ups to class. Obviously, Willie has identified a hero and role model. Our response to Willie's desire should be, "Great!" We should encourage "Air Willie" to visualize himself as the greatest basketball player, ever, and to visualize himself becoming a confident and eloquent public speaker. We should encourage Willie to develop his public speaking potential so that he may become a spokesperson for the young men who may never have his opportunity to succeed.

However, Willie has some work to do. To expand his basketball skills he needs to become a good learner, listener, and team player. When Willie begins to receive national recognition, he will have to be prepared to handle interviews, read contracts, and prepare letters of acceptance or decline to the colleges that recruit him.

1. An important exercise is to have Willie research his role model. Where did Michael Jordan go to school? What were the admission requirements (e.g., grade point average, SAT scores, etc.)? What courses did he take? What were his aspirations as a young man? What newspaper and magazine articles have been written about him? What type of son and family man is he? What type of character and integrity does he have?

2. Willie can research the history of basketball and the NBA. He can develop an all-time best team. Have him prepare a written report and verbal presentation describing each player and the attributes they bring to the team.

3. Willie is convinced that he will make it into the NBA, and we are too! Once "Air Willie" is ready for the

NBA, he will have to interview agents, attorneys, accountants, investment bankers, insurance specialists, etc. Have him prepare questions for these interviews. Perform role playing with Willie interviewing students who aspire toward these professions.

4. Get another young man who aspires to become a journalist, movie producer, television commentator, etc., and have him interview Willie for the following:

    a. College admission.

    b. Professional recruitment.

    c. Contract negotiations.

5. Willie will have to prepare himself for life after basketball. What type of business would he like to own? How will he prepare for the possibility of NBA team ownership? How will he prepare for the opportunities of becoming a sports commentator or news analyst? How will he develop the leadership skills to become a professional, college, or high school coach? What type of example will he set for our young men?

6. Discuss the career options surrounding his goal.

7. By allowing Willie to retain his goal, we simply work with him to understand and to develop himself for achievement in the areas leading up to and following a career in basketball. If Willie beats the odds and does make it into the NBA, he will have been introduced to the many things that will confront him as a professional athlete. If Willie does not make it into the Pros, we will have introduced him to an assortment of other career options while maintaining his enthusiasm and motivation for learning. This is a classic example of "a glass half full or half empty."

To me, competitive doesn't mean 'hating to lose,' it doesn't mean doing a bunch of talking. Being competitive means working your Butt off. If you're saying you're competitive, and you don't work, you're just talking.

– Jim Brown

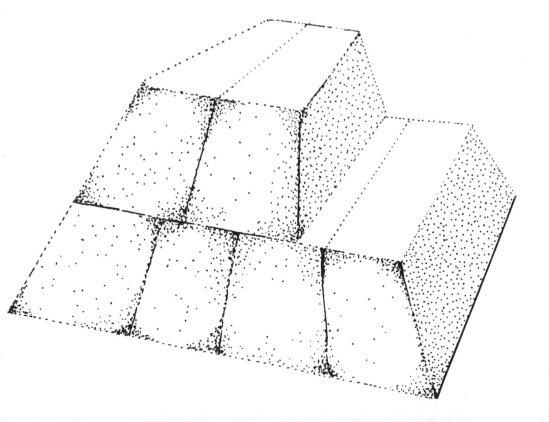

Block 6

VISUALIZATION

The sixth block of our pyramid deals with the concept of visualization. The ability to "see" something before it has physically manifested itself. Many of our young men never make it out of the ghettos of America. They never make it onto the "high road of life" because they don't "see" the opportunities available to them. They never overcome their sense of hopelessness and despair because they cannot see themselves getting there.

Martin Luther King, Jr. in one of his famous speeches eloquently said, "I've been to the mountain top, I've seen the promised land." Too many of our young men are forever stuck in the valley of despondency and desperation, forever struggling to survive; their dreams extending no further than the next day. We can begin to place our young men on the high road of life only by empowering them to pull themselves up out of the valley. We must lift them up so that they can "see the mountain top."

To help our young men visualize achievement we must help them experience success. Herein lies the problem for many of our parents and teachers. Many of our parents and teachers have become tired and frustrated from their constant battles with the multitude of complex problems plaguing our schools, homes, and communities. Remember in block four, Teacher/Parent Expectations, we examined that by focusing our attention on getting our young men to sit still in class, or simply getting out of the house and going to school we were lowering our expectations. As we lower our own expectations, we cannot help our young men *see* extraordinary achievement.

If we can get them to visualize getting straight A's or becoming a great author, doctor, lawyer, educator, or businessman we can help them to experience the smaller goals leading to achieving the extraordinary goals. By helping our young men to visualize straight A's, we can focus their energies on achieving the smaller goal of getting one A. By helping a young man to visualize becoming a great author, we can focus his energy on the smaller goal of reading one book. When our young men are visualizing climbing to the mountain top the smaller steps of climbing are not nearly as intimidating.

EXERCISE #11

Set aside some quiet time in the morning at school and in the evening at home. Have your young men close their eyes and focus on their goals. Encourage them to see themselves achieving their goals and feel themselves standing in victory.

Parents should have their son(s) include their goals in their nightly prayers. Parents should also join their son(s) in prayer in affirming their goals. Help them to visualize overcoming the obstacles and challenges in their lives.

1. Close your eyes.

2. Focus on your ultimate goal.

3. See yourself there, feel the success, and taste the victory.

4. Focus on one of the smaller goals; one of the things that you must do today to move one step closer to your goal.

5. See yourself accomplishing this smaller goal.

6. Reinforce this exercise by gathering books, magazines, newspaper articles, films, and videos that provide visual images of their goals.

7. Repeat the following affirmation:

A Pledge To Myself

Today I pledge to be
 the best possible me
No matter how good I am
 I know that I can become better

Today I pledge to build
 on the work of yesterday
Which will lead me
 into the rewards of tomorrow

Today I pledge to feed
 my mind: knowledge, understanding and wisdom
 my body: strength, and
 my spirit: faith

Today I pledge to reach
 new goals
 new challenges, and
 new horizons

Today I pledge to listen
 to the beat of my drummer
who leads me onward
 in search of my dreams

Today I pledge to believe in me

 © *Mychal Wynn*

Through visualization we are encouraged to dream; through dreaming we establish extraordinary goals; through continuing encouragement of our ability to achieve these extraordinary goals we develop plans; through planning, the steps needed to achieve our goals become tangible; each step identified in our plan becomes a smaller goal; and finally, through achieving the smaller goals within our plan we gain the confidence that we do in fact have the power to achieve our dreams.

We can help our young men to set and visualize extraordinary goals by providing them with the opportunity to see, touch, and taste their goals. If our young men want to move into an estate with a butler, maid, and chauffeur we can show them pictures and videos that help them to visualize the possibilities. We can make arrangements with a bus company to tour the homes of the "Rich and Famous." If our young men want to become great speakers, we can show them videos of great speakers and play for them audio cassettes of great speeches. We can bring some of our out-standing community leaders and preachers into our classrooms to talk about the spirit that moves them when they speak. If our young men aspire to become doctors, lawyers, educators, or stock brokers, we can arrange for them to visit hospitals, courts, col-leges, and the Stock Exchange.

As we laid into place block one, Cultural Understanding, we discussed the idea that many of our young men aspire toward athletic careers. They believe that those opportunities are within their reach. But, the scope of their dreams will broaden if they believe that there are other extraordinary opportunities available to them. If they can see themselves achieving other dreams; if they can see themselves standing on the mountain top;   if we con-stantly introduce them to the physical manifestations of their dreams our young men will develop the ability to visualize great things for themselves.

91

EXERCISE #12

1. Begin to set goals for and to visualize extraordinary achievement (e.g., straight A's; outstanding oratorical recitations, great musical and dance performances; clear, strong, and articulate expressions of thoughts and ideas, etc.).

2. Make the following questions part of routine dialogue with your students or son:

   a. What do you want to be?

   b. Begin to affirm this regularly by saying such things as; "You have the power to become the greatest_____ ever." "What are you going to do when you become that?"

   c. Close your eyes and see yourself there.

   d. Now tell me what you see?

   e. What did you learn in school today that will help you get there?

   f. Great! You're going to need to know that to become a great . . .

3. Have our young men regularly read books about their goals and share or report on what they've read.

4. Get them in the habit of discussing their thoughts, ideas, and opinions.

5. Introduce our young men to books about great African-American men who have achieved the things that they want to achieve and discuss with them how their lives compare with the lives of those men.

6. Ask them to visualize the success that these men experienced.

7. Identify positive quotations and poems that will help
    them to visualize and affirm their goals. Display these
    throughout your home/classroom (e.g., on the
    refrigerator, in the bathroom, his bedroom, walls, etc.)
    and periodically ask our young men to recite them.

*Words spoken without meaning have no tentacles.
They float endlessly, bouncing here and there, restless
pieces of the spirit; sent out without any mission or
specific destination, landing no where and serving no
purpose, except to diminish the spirit of the speaker.*

– J.C. Bell

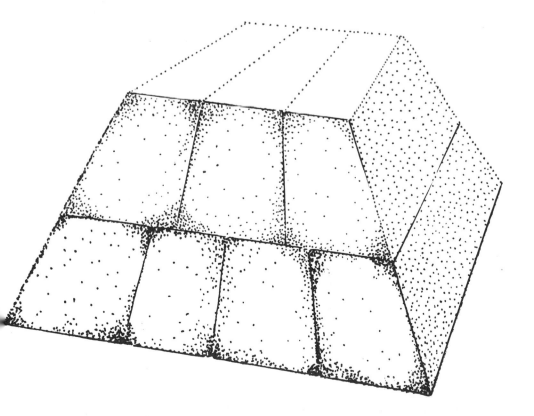

Block 7

AFFIRMATION

In many African-American churches we are taught the biblical principle that there is life-giving power in the power of the tongue. We can speak life unto our lives, or death unto our lives! This means that we can affirm success or we can affirm failure by what we say. Our children, particularly our young men, often say negative and discouraging things to each other. In many homes, siblings say more discouraging things to each other than positive and encouraging things. The media highlights many more negative things pertaining to our young men than they do their positive achievements and potential.

Everywhere we turn there are negative events and negative statistics discussing the negative behavior of our young men! Why should we be surprised that so many of our young men are walking the streets of America helpless and hopeless, discouraged and defeated, frustrated and angry? Everywhere they turn people are affirming their failure. To those who say, "We're only acknowledging the problems," I say that if you're not affirming solutions, you're only affirming the perpetuation of the problems!

Our young men begin life with wide-eyed wonder and bright inquisitive minds. They see the world as their playground, full of joy and laughter. Our young men don't know the hopelessness of their situation until we affirm it for them. Our young men don't know that they're not supposed to succeed in life until we affirm the probability of their failing. Our pyramid is being constructed on a solid foundation. We have laid our blocks into place with strong, loving, compassionate hands. Our young men are becoming more powerful. They are visualizing success.

This seventh block of our pyramid will have them affirming success. It will empower them to speak life unto their lives. When those around them are speaking of the hopelessness of their situation, they will be empowered to speak of the possibilities. Throughout history, great coaches have used affirmations to inspire and motivate their teams to victory. We have all witnessed teams that appeared to be beaten and defeated at half time. Yet they came out for the second half with a passion and intensity that carried them on to victory. These coaches have learned how to motivate their players during the half-time pep talk. They are successful at getting their players to visualize success and to affirm victory.

Our young men are at half time. The game is not over. We can prepare them for victory in the second half. Our attitude can determine their altitude! Our homes and classrooms can enhance the spirit of learning by having our young men affirm their success daily. These verbal declarations of self-esteem, self-confidence, winning, and succeeding in life are powerful. When confronted with the troubles and obstacles that they experience on a daily basis, the time set aside for affirming success may give them the strength, courage, and confidence to endure.

Dr. Crystal Kuykendall in her keynote address before the Wholistic Institute tells the story of "Lying Lewis."

"In the seventh grade I had a student called 'Lying Lewis.' Everybody had warned me about Lewis. And when Lewis entered my classroom, I immediately knew that they were right! This boy could lie. And he was good too!

I started telling Lewis that anybody who knows intuitively what to say and make people believe it had a special gift.

I told Lewis that he would make a great politician! I wanted Lewis to know that there was a high road consistent with his special gifts.

Every time that I called on Lewis I would say, 'Assemblyman Hester, or Congressman Hester, or Senator Hester.' I would bring Lewis into the classroom discussions by saying, 'Senator Hester, do you have an opinion on this?' It got to be so good to Lewis that he corrected me one day and said, 'Call me President Hester!'"

Dr. Kuykendall went on to say that she continued encouraging Lewis for a couple of years before she lost track of him. She would discover some years later that "Lying Lewis" would become Attorney Lewis, practicing law in Newark, New Jersey. Dr. Kuykendall, through affirming Lewis's greatness, would put this young man on the high road of life!

We can empower all of our young men by identifying and affirming their special gifts. But to do this requires changing our attitudes and our perceptions of our young men. All that the other teachers saw in Lewis was a lying and conniving young man who couldn't be trusted and had to be watched! But Dr. Kuykendall saw a special gift with extraordinary potential. If we are to stop the seemingly endless flow our young men dropping out of our schools and dropping into drugs and gangs, we must begin to affirm a better life for them. We must begin to help them to see their special gifts and their extraordinary potential.

Despite prejudice and racism, ignorance and bigotry, there are doors of opportunities that we can empower them to open. We must affirm that the opportunities exist and that they are capable of taking advantage of them. Each day we should affirm with them such positive affirmations as this personal adaptation of the poem "Born To Win."

Born To Win

I was born to become an Eagle
to spread my wings and fly
with strength and perseverance
I'll continue reaching toward the sky

I was born to become a Lion
to stand tall, proud, and free
my faith and determination
casting a light for all to see

And like a Ram I'll stand on the mountain top
greeting the dawn of each new day
prepared to meet whatever obstacles
that should dare to block my way

I will stand before the rising Sun
with a sense of pride that stands the test
accepting challenges, I will dare to dream
I will dare to become the best

©Mychal Wynn

EXERCISE #13

By having our young men identify their goals in extraordinary terms we can begin to help them to see themselves achieving those goals. We must now help them to empower their spirits by affirming their greatness. The following affirmation should become a part of their regular routine at home and at school.

1. I am going to <u>YOUR GOAL</u> (e.g., become one of the world's great motivational speakers).

2. I know that I have the power to do that.

3. I know that there are many things that I must do to get there, but I know that I am capable of getting there.

4. I know that few things that are worthwhile come easy and that few things that are easy are worthwhile.

5. I know that I will make mistakes, but that will not discourage me from striving for perfection.

6. I know there will be times when I have only done pretty good, but that will not discourage me from striving for excellence.

7. I know that if I don't quit, I cannot fail.

8. I am going to <u>YOUR GOAL</u> (e.g., become a great speaker).

9. I know that I have the power to do that.

The major piece of information I absorbed after twelve years of public education was that I was a problem, inferior, uneducable and a victim. And, as a victim, I began to see the world through the eyes of a victim.

– Haki R. Madhubuti

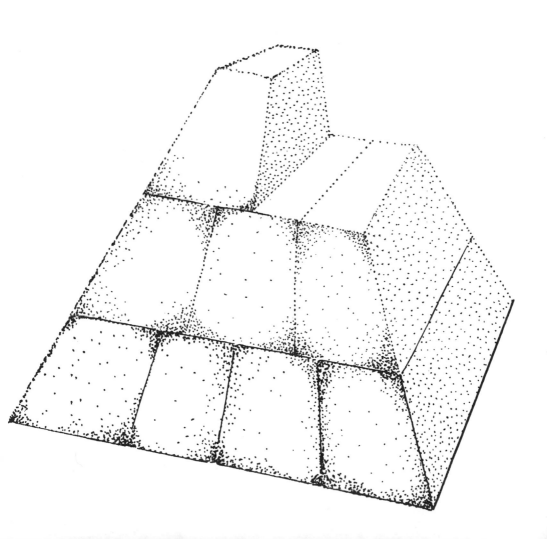

Block 8

INTEGRATE CURRICULUM/HOME

In workshops presenting the concepts that we've examined thus far, I always discover some participants who are convinced that the ideas have merit; however, their situation is different. They respond: "Mr. Wynn, I can see this working for some students, but my situation is different."

"You see Mr. Wynn, the children in the community where I teach have no motivation."

"They don't have any role models and I don't think that any of this will work on them."

These teachers are failing because of their inability to captivate the attention of the young men whom they are responsible for teaching.

When our young men become bored and disinterested in what the teacher is teaching, we simply assume that the fault lies with the student and not with the method of teaching. Everything that we've examined, thus far, has demonstrated how to integrate an Afrocentric approach into our curriculum; how to develop culturally-based lesson plans, parenting and teaching styles, that develop confidence in our young men so that what we're teaching is consistent with the achievement of their goals. If we are successful in this regard, our young men will become motivated and our classrooms and our homes will begin to represent symbols of excellence.

Our challenge as parents and teachers is to create an environment in which our young men are motivated to become empowered to develop the skills that they need to make positive and constructive choices in their lives.

- In laying our first block, we discussed developing teaching techniques based on cultural understanding.

- In laying our second block, we discussed the importance of getting our young men to buy in to a standard of behavior and code of conduct.

- In laying our third block, we discussed the importance of establishing personal responsibility.

- In laying our fourth block, we discussed the double-edged sword of teacher/parent expectations. We can carve positive or negative, high or low expectations for our young men.

- In laying our fifth block, we discussed establishing extraordinary goals and preparing our young men for success.

- In laying our sixth block, we discussed visualizing success; being able to see the mountain top.

- In laying our seventh block, we discussed how to speak life unto our lives, the power of the tongue and how our young men can affirm their success.

Our success at laying these blocks into place results from our own enhanced understanding of African-American males, their culture, the culture of their communities, and the African-American influence on goal setting and achievement. These strategies, teaching/parenting styles, and techniques are all designed to empower our young men to succeed.

When our young men exhibit their extraordinary energy levels, they are labeled as hyperactive. When they speak loudly and play roughly, they are labeled as wild and coming from poor home environments. Yet, expanding our cultural understanding leads us to recognize that many of our young men are drawn into competitive sports that harness their aggressive and extraordinary energy. They naturally bond with athletic coaches who provide male role models who encourage their pursuit of excellence and provide discipline and direction. Our young men participate in more interactive team sports (e.g., basketball, baseball, football) than individual and non-interactive team sports (e.g., tennis, golf, gymnastics, swimming). With this cultural understanding, we should make our classrooms and homes more team oriented, disciplined, and focused. Reinforcing the idea that it's great to have a superstar, but that it's the whole team that wins the championship.

Understanding that African-American men have a rich tradition of oral communication, we must solicit more verbal responses in our classrooms. Even in subjects like math, science, and social studies we can enhance the thinking skills and heighten the interests of our young men by requiring explanations of problems and solutions. High-spirited, high-energy discussions will have a better chance of capturing the attention of our young men. If you've ever seen African-American men speak professionally, you've noticed that they move their bodies and their hands. They raise and lower their voices for emphasis. They code switch between standard and "Black English." The truly good ones have the unique ability to identify with a cross-spectrum of people from young to old, rich to poor, uneducated to professional, using code switching for emphasis: "Y'all know what I mean?"

Challenge your young men to develop a rap about history, math, and science that will bring the subjects to life. This merges the skills and talents that they want to develop with the material that the teacher wants to cover. Getting them to move from their seats to the front of the class to explain answers will help to keep them awake and focused and avoid their becoming restless and disinterested. By developing a supportive and encouraging environment in your classroom, you will provide them the opportunity of overcoming shyness, enhancing their public speaking ability and developing their presentation skills. Encouraging them to speak loudly and clearly will help them to better and more forcefully articulate their ideas, feelings, and opinions. Continue to integrate your increased cultural understanding of our young men and their communities into your teaching strategies.

Janice Hale-Benson, in *Black Children: Their Roots, Culture, and Learning Styles*, points to research performed by Akpan Ebsen which suggests that "The African modes of child-rearing give rise to the development of humane attitudes and the care syndrome. Unlike Western child-rearing, African socialization emphasizes the closeness of man-to-man. Physical and psychological closeness is reinforced by encouragement of body contact between people." Our young men like to be touched, hugged, slapped on the back, and spoken to face-to-face, and eye-to-eye. Janice Hale-Benson also points out that, "The problems the teacher had with the Black children seemed to stem from a cultural mismatch between the teacher and child."

Utilizing what we've learned, we must alter our teaching styles and strategies to motivate, captivate, and inspire our African-American male students.

- Don't teach from the front of the room; be mobile.
- Don't embarrass our young men in front of their peers.
- If they don't know the answer, spend as much time as you need to have them discover the answer for themselves.
- Don't develop your seating patterns by alphabets or based on test scores.

Most classrooms are set up in an auditorium seating pattern (Eurocentric style learning). In these classrooms, we encourage and reward individual achievement. Eventually, we further separate the fast learners and high achievers from the slower

108

learners and lower achievers. Many teachers begin to direct their questions to the high achievers to keep the class moving so that it won't be slowed down by the slower learners or sidetracked by those young men viewed as having behavior problems. This type of classroom perpetuates a caste system. We create the feeling among our young men, and within our community, that some of us are more important than others. That lowers the self-esteem of the one group, while encouraging those developing the skills to enhance the image and substance of our community to, in fact, separate themselves from the community.

Roy Weaver, in *Beyond Identity: Education and the Future Role of Black Americans,* points out that "The social climate developed in the school is associated with the effectiveness of the socialization process. In other words, the way the teacher structures his relations with the children and their relations with each other establishes a behavioral model for them. Accordingly, the organization of the classroom must be examined in relation to the growth and development of the children."

As previously stated, African-American children, nationwide, while representing only 17 percent of all children in public schools, comprise over 41 percent of all children in special education. Of the African-American children in special education, 85 percent of them are African-American males. African-American males represent the greatest percentage, nationally, of suspensions (37 percent). Many of our young men are being "misplaced" in special education as a result of poorly-organized classrooms. Remember the first block of our pyramid, Cultural Understanding.

The work group style of classroom organization (family-style learning) can encourage individual responsibility through peer pressure. Work group classroom organization is an integral part of our holistic approach to teaching our young men. We can establish individual responsibilities that are reinforced through peer pressure. The typical American classroom is a competitive experience where students are encouraged to compete against each other for the best grades, the teacher's attention, the best test scores, etc.

Many of our young men being placed in learning disability and behavioral disorder classes can be saved through work group implementation. Their individual levels of responsibility would be tied to the values and norms of the work group. We would replace individual competition with work group or team competition. Good teams will still have their superstars; however, the less talented players can experience the joy of victory and extraordinary achievement resulting from a team effort. This holistic approach to teaching our young men works to assist the higher achievers in developing leadership skills, an enhanced appreciation for their special gifts, enhanced self-esteem, and a greater sensitivity to the problems and needs of their classmates and the community at-large. The slower learners are made to feel as important as the high achievers, thus raising their self-esteem. Through the inherently competitive nature of our young men, the slower learners are encouraged to work harder to rival the success of the higher achievers.

The students who are good at math begin to bond with those students who are good at science and those students who are good at social studies. Working together reinforces the idea that our community requires that our young men work together to redefine its future. Our young men will begin to develop a multitude of individual skills and an appreciation for the unique skills and talents of each other. This prepares our young men for the complexities of getting along with, and working together with, people of differing skill levels, backgrounds, and opinions in the post-school world.

To understand the importance of this type of learning and bonding experience, one need only to look at the large numbers of young, successful African-American professionals who have few long-standing relationships with the people whom they went to school. The more talented students, through traditional class-rooms, were pushed toward individual achievement. They found themselves leaving the slow ones behind and were encouraged to leave the community in pursuit of the "American Dream." Our communities have continued to deteriorate as the most talented and most capable within our communities, have left. Many of our classrooms are set up in a manner not only inconsistent with the learning styles of African-American children, but in a manner inconsistent with how businesses with whom they will eventually be seeking employment are set up.

As major companies seek to establish greater quality control; increase employee productivity; develop faster responses to their constantly changing, competitive environments, various types of employee work groups are being developed. These employee work groups (i.e., task forces, focus groups, project teams) bring together employees from different parts of the company, with different educational backgrounds and skill levels, to work together to identify and resolve problems and issues confronting the company.

To succeed in almost any endeavor, it is critically important to network and work with people of differing backgrounds and skill levels. Networking further helps to strengthen the bond between our young men and perhaps will even save lives in our urban communities by not pitting one side of the community against the other. A work group methodology will help our future leaders to develop a greater sense of responsibility to the community and will reinforce within our young men that we are all in this together.

Wade Nobles, in *Infusion of African and African-American Content in the School Curriculum*, points out: "By infusing African and African-American content in the curricula, we, in effect, reaffirm the inalienable right of African people to (1) exist as a people; (2) contribute to the forward flowing process of human civilization (as contributors and not debtors) and (3) share with

111

as well as shape the world (reality) in response to our own energy and spirit."

EXERCISE #14

1. Take two sheets of paper. Put your name at the top of one and the name of a young man that you would like to reach at the top of the other.

2. Write down the following on each sheet of paper:
    - Personal goals
    - Personal background
    - Describe the household
    - Estimate the household income
    - Describe the support group (friends, community, parents, etc.)
    - Describe perceived opportunities
    - Describe the history of successful personal experiences
    - Describe any extraordinary goal achievement

3. These two sheets represent the two people who make up your team. You must develop a strategy to merge the talents, backgrounds, and experiences in order to achieve a common goal. To integrate our pyramid into the life of this young man is to infuse our newly-found understanding of his life, including everything that we can that will empower him to succeed.

Passion is not friendly. It is arrogant, superbly contemptuous of all that is not itself, and, as the very definition of passion implies the impulse to freedom, it has a mighty intimidating power. It contains a challenge. It contains an unspeakable hope.

– James Baldwin

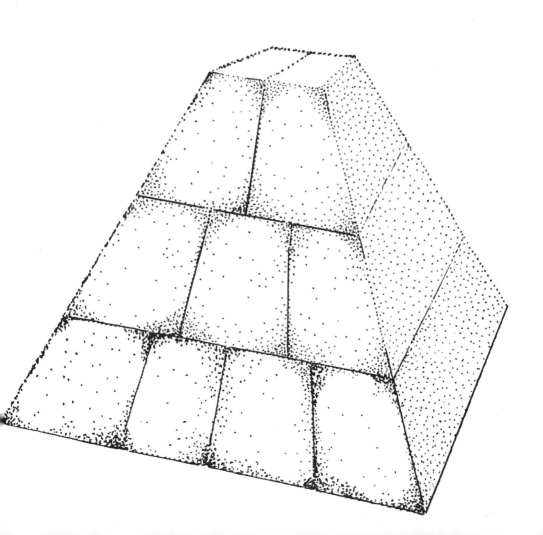

Block 9

A PASSION FOR EXCELLENCE

Our pyramid is a beacon of hope for our community. Each block has been laid into place with caring and compassionate hands. We have identified some of the cultural characteristics of our young men as being humanistic, gravitating toward team sports and group activities. We know that many of our young men suffer from low self-esteem and feel powerless to change their situations. Yet we know our young men to be verbally and physically aggressive with tremendous energy levels.

Many American classrooms fail our young men because they fail to harness their tremendous energies. We are a very high-energy and passionate people from our music to our dance to our tremendous oratory. Our young men, who have proven to be extraordinarily competitive, will begin to develop a passion for excellence as we harness and focus their energy on goal achievement.

Many schools have oral language programs in which teachers work with our young men in preparing them for oratorical recitations. Many teachers work very diligently to help our young men memorize the words. Yet they fail to develop the spirit and passion for the presentation. They fail to help the young men visualize and affirm the great oratorical styles of Martin Luther King, Jr., Frederick Douglass, or Jesse Jackson. Creating a passion for excellence is to propel our young men toward the very pinnacle of achievement. The oratorical recitation should be performed at a level that uplifts and motivates the audience. Reaching out and touching the spirit of all who bear witness to this extraordinary presentation. All the energy of the basketball court and football field; all the passion and aggressiveness of "The Dozens"; all the energy and power of our young men's loud and intimidating verbal skills should be harnessed into this presentation!

This is excellence. This is empowerment. This is what our young men are capable of. Our pyramid stands tall. The mortar of love and understanding provides strong, indestructible bonding. The foundation is laid. Our homes, our classrooms, and our schools have developed environments that encourage learning, dreaming, goal setting, character building, and achievement into which we can inject the spirit of excellence. Everything that we do, say, and teach should reinforce the spirit of excellence. Our code of conduct and our standard of behavior must reinforce the spirit of excellence.

Our young men must be taught to walk tall, stand strong, and speak clearly. Their handshakes must be strong and confident. We must teach them to speak with confidence and conviction. We must encourage them to excel by raising our own expectations. A quest for excellence means that "A" students should get A's and "B" students should get better. It means that it is unacceptable for any student to fail. If any student fails, it must not be because his parents and teachers have failed him.

A quest for excellence means that it is not acceptable for our young men to introduce themselves with their heads bowed, speaking in weak, failing voices. A quest for excellence means that every parent and teacher should marvel at the pride, confidence, self-assurance, and dignity displayed by their sons and students. When we look into the mirror of our community, we see our own reflection.

EXERCISE #15

1. Gather a group of young men, ideally eight to ten.

2. The poem that follows: "What Manner of Men are We," may be photocopied for use in this exercise. Distribute a copy to each young man highlighting from one to three consecutive lines on each copy (i.e., the first young man has the first three lines highlighted, the next young man has the next two lines, and so on).

3. After you've highlighted all the lines in the poem, work with this group to prepare an oral recitation as follows:

    a. Let the young men recite their lines without any coaching. (Usually, they will hold their heads down, tap their feet, and are barely audible in their presentation.)

    b. Recite the poem for them. (This is where you have to use expression in your voice. Place emphasis on certain words; inject anger into such words as "in the boxing rings"; inject pain into such words as "castration and degradation.")

    c. Now have them repeat the poem. (See if someone steps forward with some clarity and authority. When that person does, respond "Yes, that's it, put some power into it!")

4. After you've repeated this poem several times, you should begin to witness the following:

    a. Their competitive nature begins to show as they try to become louder, more forceful, more emotional than each other.

    b. Someone will ask, "Can I do his part?"

c. When several people have done well and someone makes a mistake, they will begin to exert peer pressure. (Be sure to keep this positively focused.)

d. Someone will step forward and say, "I know it all. Can I do the whole thing?"

5. As you continue to coach them, encourage them to step forward when it's their turn. Encourage them to raise their voices; inject some emotion; move their arms; and dramatically express themselves (harness their passion).

6. Encourage them to establish eye contact with you while they're reciting their parts.

With continued practice and encouragement, you will begin to see:

- Increased self-pride and self-confidence.
- They will begin to articulate words that they've never articulated before.
- They will look forward to taking center stage.
- They will want to do more poems and presentations.

What Manner of Men are We . . .

What manner of men are we
    who move gracefully and swiftly
    along the football fields and basketball courts of the world
Constantly pounding or being pounded
    in the boxing rings of Atlantic City and the inner city
Robbed from the bosom of Mother Africa
    and the richness of South Africa
Having journeyed from the mountain top to the selling block
Experiencing over 300 years of
    castration and degradation,
    every indignity and humiliation
Yet continuing to grow tall and strong
Creating a history rich in achievement
We discovered blood plasma and the cotton gin
    gas masks and harpoons, baby carriages and traffic lights
    machines to plant seeds and machines to stretch shoes
We were the first to die
    in the struggle for this country's independence
    and the first to successfully perform open heart surgery
We are Martin and Marcus, Malcolm and Benjamin
    Frederick and W.E.B., Jesse and Booker T.
We are Jesse, Jackie, and Joe
    the Big E, and the Big O
We are Clyde the Glide and Earl the Pearl
We are the Watusi and the Mandingo
There are none bigger, none better
    none taller, and none stronger
When we have it all together
That's what manner of men we are!

© Mychal Wynn

This exercise is not intimidating because they begin as a team (family-styled learning). They don't have to take center stage all by themselves. They have peer group support to perform well. They are not as intimidated by the new words because everyone is at the same disadvantage. This exercise may become one of the most powerful and positive experiences, ever, for these young men. We have taken an understanding of their culture (an oral tradition of communication, team and tribal participation, and high energy) and placed them into a competitive, team oriented exercise. I've prepared young men using this exercise from grades K through 12. I've had them present this poem before the entire student body. I've sat in the audience and watched them on stage while their "homeboys" sat stunned at how confident and articulate they stood before their peers. This simple exercise highlights, strengthens, and reinforces our natural oratory skills.

It promotes the spirit of excellence through dramatic impassioned presentation. It provides a bonding between the young men engaging in the statement of who they are. It channels their naturally-powerful energy into positive, powerful language. It uplifts the spirit of the young men who perform it and of the students who hear it. It builds upon their competitive team spirit in reaching for excellence. It allows our slow learners to compete on the same platform with our faster learners. It combines our less powerful with those who are more powerful. It makes a personal statement about our history and our rightful place among the best in the world.

Kunta Kente was the product of a society that held its young in high esteem and developed a network of role models and functional institutions to assist him in his social development. Until the day he was attacked and kidnaped by slavers, Kunta Kente had been raised in a fashion that clearly defined who he was, his responsibility to his parents, relatives, and community, and his sense of manhood.

– Useni Eugene Perkins

Block 10

EMPOWERMENT

The final block of our pyramid is ready to be laid into place. Our foundation is solid, our mortar is strong, and our young men are becoming empowered. Our young men are beginning to believe in themselves. In doing so, they are gaining newly-found respect for themselves and their community. We can hear it in their voices as they articulate their dreams with pride, dignity, and conviction. They are becoming examples for their communities that: "We are only limited by the scope of our dreams!"

As we plant the seeds of empowerment we will give birth to the spirit of entrepreneurship. A spirit of confidence and pride in doing for yourself. A spirit that must become embedded within the consciousness of our young men if the true emancipation of the African-American community in general, and the African-American male in particular is to come about. An emancipation that breaks the chains that have bound our young men into believing themselves powerless and their situations hopeless.

The spirit of entrepreneurship provides he who has it with an undeniable advantage over he who does not. The entrepreneur sees opportunities where others see only problems. The entrepreneur accepts responsibility while others make excuses. The entrepreneur is constantly studying, learning, working, and building while others are complaining and allowing that which has been built to decay. The entrepreneur takes advantage of

127

opportunities and develops solutions without waiting for others to provide for his needs.

Embedding the spirit of entrepreneurship within the consciousness of our young men will empower them to see their potential and their ability to shape their destinies. It is this spirit that will enable our young men to view employment as a means and not an end. It is this spirit that will enable them to project the confidence and self-assurance needed to become employed; to advance and to learn while employed; and to apply their knowledge in building their own businesses so that they may become employers. It is this spirit that will empower our young men to become the future leaders of our communities; loving husbands and strong fathers.

I have provided you with a framework for empowerment, yet as parents and teachers your task is much greater. Now that you are verbally and mentally affirming success for our young men, you must still develop the daily lesson plans for your students and raise your sons in a manner that will help them to achieve the best in themselves.

To maintain an empowered consciousness in our young men, we must empower their minds through reading and diligent study. Our young men should be reading, writing, and speaking about the richness of our heritage and developing visions of our future. This empowered consciousness will enable our young men to become men of thought; men of action; men of conviction; men of purpose; men of principle; men of strength; and men of courage. To empower our young men is to harness their tremendous energy so that they grow mentally, as well as in stature.

James Weldon Johnson stated: "Every race and every nation should be judged by the best it has been able to produce, not by the worst." Our challenge as parents and teachers is to create the best environment in our homes and our classrooms; to empower our young men to achieve the best that they are capable of achieving.

We must not forget that we are engaged in a battle for the souls of our children. Our urban communities have become so violent and so full of those who would destroy our young men, that we must be forever mindful of the dangerous road that our young men must travel. As we empower them we must empower ourselves to provide for them a safe and secure environment in our homes and in our schools. We must consciously uplift, edify, and encourage our young men in our homes, schools, and churches, constantly affirming their potential for extraordinary achievement. We must put on our armor and defend them from uncaring teachers and administrators, abusive parents and law enforcement officials, and the gangs and violence that threatens to destroy our communities.

Through your guidance, our young men must become sufficiently empowered to make life-saving decisions to avoid drugs, to turn away from crime and violence, and to denounce the lure of street gangs. We must help our young men to see the extraordinary potential in their lives and to develop confidence and self-assurance. Perhaps they will begin to overcome the darkness and despair of our inner cities with a vision and hope of excellence. Your application of the strategies outlined in this book will inspire our young men to greatness. It is a powerful thing to touch someone's life; to know that you've said or done something that has helped them to become a better person. Isn't that what teaching and parenting is all about?

W.E.B. DuBois wrote: "I believe in pride of race and lineage and self: in pride of self so deep as to scorn injustice to other selves. Especially do I believe in the Negro Race: in the beauty of its genius, the sweetness of its soul, and its strength in that meekness which shall inherit this turbulent earth."

The success in empowering our young men to achieve their goals is articulated in the poem: "The Spirit Within You."

Our young men should realize their potential to stand in the light of their dreams as expressed in the words of the poem: "Overcoming Darkness."

The Spirit Within You

The magnificence of the Universe
    Its beauty and energy
    Its wisdom and understanding
Are one with the spirit
dwelling within you

The stars are beacons
Beckoning you onward
    challenging you to dream
    encouraging you to believe

No journey is so far
    that the Spirit cannot lead you
No journey is so great
    that the Spirit cannot strengthen you

Without the Spirit
    the smallest obstacle appears insurmountable

With the Spirit
    you are powerful and unyielding
    diligent and determined
Capable of becoming
    all that you were created to be

© Mychal Wynn

Overcoming Darkness

There is a great wall
        surrounding each of us
invisible, yet firm
each brick solidly joined
blocking the light
        challenging us to dream
to believe in things unseen
to dare reach for things unreachable

The wall is unyielding
splattered with the blood and sweat
        of those who dared
cemented stronger
        by those who quit
It has shattered the dreams
of the most optimistic
Yet the strength of this wall
        is an illusion
destroyed by unwavering faith
each brick giving way
        to a ray of hope
The more you persevere
the more it crumbles before you
Standing on your faith
        enables you
to stand triumphantly in the light
Where you discover
        it is the illusion of failure
        that darkens the minds
of those without faith

© *Mychal Wynn*

The empowerment of the African-American Male in America should not be intimidating or frightening. It should be sought after and applauded. Successful teaching and successful parenting produces successful young men and women. The true measurement of America is the success of her people . . . all of her people.

He who starts behind in the great race of life must forever remain behind or run faster than the man in front.

– Benjamin E. Mays

Real education means to inspire people to live more abundantly, to learn to begin with life as they find it and make it better.

– Carter G. Woodson

Time is neutral and does not change things. With courage and initiative, leaders change things.

– Jesse Jackson

When I discover who I am, I'll be free.

– Ralph Ellison

Schoolhouses do not teach themselves — piles of brick and mortar and machinery do not send out men. It is strengthened by long study and thought, that breathes the real breath of life into boys and girls and makes them human.

— W.E.B. DuBois

Epilogue

When I entered kindergarten, firmly rooted in my culture, I met a jolly teacher whose warm smile and tight hugs reminded me of my mother. This jolly old educator took me as I was, tattered clothes and nappy hair; full lips and broad nose; high energy and inquisitive mind. When I said, "I ain't got none," she told me, "I don't have any." The way she said it made it sound right although she never criticized me for saying it differently.

As I journeyed through school, I met other teachers who made me feel proud of myself. They never told me that being Black was bad or that my "Black English" was wrong. They just told me that there was another way to speak so that other people could understand me. When I came to school "leanin'," with my pants hanging low and my shirt hanging out, they didn't tell me that I was disgraceful, just that there was a standard of behavior and a code of conduct more befitting my royal heritage.

When they taught me math and science, they told me of the Africans who were the first great mathematicians, astrologers, scientists, and philosophers. When they taught me pride in myself, they told me of the strength, conviction, and principles of Booker T. Washington, George Washington Carver, Martin Luther King, Jr., Malcolm X, and Paul Robeson. They always told me that I was capable of overcoming any obstacle; that I would experience prejudice and ignorance, but that I must never feel that I was not entitled to the very best that life had to offer.

They always told me that the homeless and helpless brothers were not always that way; that there was a time when the world marveled at the architectural, historical, and artistic achievements of Africans; that the beauty of African women and the strength, courage, and leadership of African men had inspired cultures throughout the world. They always told me that I could become a great business leader; that I could become an employer—not just an employee; that I could shape the face of my community—not just wait for others to decide my fate.

Yes, beginning with that jolly old educator, I have been taught that my lineage did not begin in the ghetto of America but at the beginning of civilization. I have been empowered with courage and confidence, cultural awareness and compassion, principles and conviction, diligence and determination. I have been loved and nurtured, disciplined and educated, taught self-respect and respect for others. Those who love me have placed me on the high road of life. I have been empowered to succeed!

Now that each block of our pyramid has been laid into place, we confront yet another challenge. Now that we have begun to empower our young men to believe in themselves and to begin to reach for extraordinary goals, there is more. Integral to the holistic rearing and teaching of our young men is "The Rite of Passage," representing a formal recognition of the transition from boyhood to manhood.

Nathan and Julia Hare, in *Bringing the Black Boy to Manhood: The Passage*, state: "What we need, is some way to bring the black boy to manhood, to highlight and sharpen the focus of the importance and significance of being a man. We must be in search of a way to give the black boy a sense of becoming a man, a clearer sense of self and of purpose, responsibility to his roles as father and husband, a sacredness of self and others in the context of a more attentive family and community network of adult endorsement."

In building our pyramid, the foundation is anchored by our block of Cultural Understanding. To understand the importance of "the passage," we must reflect culturally on the pre-colonial customs, rituals, and ceremonies of Africa. In Africa, there was a formal Rite of Passage for the young men of the tribe to make a ceremonial journey and accept the associated responsibilities of manhood. The African-American community has no such community-wide program. There is no formal acknowledgment of, and associated responsibilities for, recognizing manhood.

Many of our young men undergo initiation rites when entering gangs. Is this the standard of manhood that we want our young men to be measured against? This is a code of conduct that places them in direct opposition to the progress, prosperity, and rebuilding of our communities. Many of our young men undergo initiation rites when pledging fraternities in college. Pledgees are often seen barking like dogs, walking, looking, and acting in demoralizing and dehumanizing ways. Is this the most empowering, dignified, respectful, responsible way for our young men to enter manhood?

So many of our young men have an overpowering, almost addictive, need to join a group or gang that they are willing to do almost anything. A rite of passage program should elevate and edify our young boys to become men. Through a rite of passage, they should formally accept the responsibilities of manhood. They should be formally presented before the community and required to think, articulate, and display what it means to be a man. The transition from boyhood to manhood requires an awareness and acknowledgment that they represent the life-blood of the community. They are the future vanguards of our history. The fathers of our children. The leaders of our journey toward excellence in our schools, homes, churches, businesses, political offices, and communities.

The world will begin to see the African-American man differently, because through the Rite of Passage, our young men will see themselves differently. The world will begin to expect the best from African-American men, because our young men will expect excellence from themselves. The African-American men whom we have empowered, by using our pyramid, will stand as one of the Great Wonders of the World, having made the journey from hopelessness and despair to self-assurance and prosperity.

The Rite of Passage should become as common in our schools and homes as are pimples and puppy love. Our communities should come to bestow the same adulation on our young boys who become men as we do upon our athletes and movie stars. All of our young men should come to expect and eagerly anticipate their transition from boyhood to manhood.

We can, whenever and wherever we choose, successfully teach all children whose schooling is of interest to us. We already know more than we need in order to do this. Whether we do it must finally depend on how we feel about the fact that we haven't so far.

– Ron Edmonds

References

Bell, Janet Cheatham. Famous Black Quotations. Chicago, IL: Sabayt Publications, 1986.

Brookover, W., Beady, C., Flood, P., Schweitzer, J., & Wisenbaker, J. School Social Systems and Student Achievement: Schools Can Make a Difference. So. Hadley, MA: J.F. Bergin Co., distributed by Praeger Publishers, New York 1979.

Brophy, J.E., & Good, T.L. Teacher-Student Relationships: Causes and Consequences. New York, NY: Holt, Rinehart, and Winston, 1974.

Clarke, John Henrik. Can African People Save Themselves? Detroit, MI: Alkebulans, Inc., 1990

Duncan, Thelma. (PEP) Los Angeles Unified School District. Proficiency in English Program for Speaker's of 'Black English.' Los Angeles, CA.

Hale-Benson, Janice. Black Children: Their Roots, Culture, and Learning Styles. Baltimore, MD: Johns Hopkins University Press, 1986.

Hare, Nathan and Julia. Bringing the Black Boy to Manhood: The Passage. San Francisco, CA: Black Think Tank, 1985

Hilliard, Payton-Stewart, Williams. Infusion of African and African-American Content in the School Curriculum. Morristown, PA: Aaron Press, 1990.

Hood, Elizabeth F. Educating Black Students: Some Basic Issues. Detroit, MI: Detroit Educational Consultants, 1973.

Johnson/Johnson. Motivating Minority Students: Strategies that Work. Springfield, IL: Thomas Books, 1988.

Kunjufu, Jawanza. Countering the Conspiracy to Destroy Black Boys. Volumes I, II, and III. Chicago, IL: African-American Images, 1983, 1986, 1990.

Ibid. Motivating and Preparing Black Youth to Work. 1986.

Ibid. A Talk with Jawanza. 1989.

Kuykendall, Crystal. Keynote Address "The High Road To Life" Wholistic Institute. Atlanta, GA, 1991.

Madhubuti, Haki. Black Men: Obsolete, Single, Dangerous? Chicago, IL: Third World Press, 1990.

Perkins, Useni Eugene. Harvesting New Generations: The Positive Development of Black Youth. Chicago, IL: Third World Press, 1990.

Persell, C.H. Education and Inequality: The Roots and Results of Stratification in America's Schools. New York, NY: The Free Press, 1977.

Star Plan: The Portland Blueprint: Success for Students at Risk Portland, OR: Public Schools, 1989.

Robinson/Weaver, et al. Beyond Identity: Education and the Future Role of Black Americans. Ann Arbor, MI: University Microfilms, 1978.

Smith/Chunn. Black Education: A Quest for Equity and Excellence. New Brunswick, CT: Transaction Publishers, 1989

West, Earle H. The Black American and Education. Columbus, OH: Merrill Publishing, 1972.

Woodson, Carter G. The Mis-Education of the Negro. Associated Publishers: 1933.

Wynn, Mychal. Don't Quit - Inspirational Poetry. South Pasadena, CA: Rising Sun Publishing, 1990.

Films/Video Materials

ABC News (Producer). "The Eye of the Storm." New York: ABC Merchandising, Inc., Film Library, 1970.

CBS (Producer). "Marva." (From 60 Minutes.) New York: Carousel Films, Inc., 1979.

Additional copies of Mychal Wynn's Empowering African-American Males to Succeed: A Ten-Step Approach for Parents and Teachers, may be purchased at your local bookstore or by mailing this order form directly to the Publisher.

SEND TOGETHER WITH CHECK OR P.O. # TO:

RISING SUN PUBLISHING
1012 Fair Oaks Boulevard, Suite 104
South Pasadena, CA 91030
(818) 799-1999

Qty _____ X $15.95 _____

SUBTOTAL _____ $ _____

CA Residents SALES TAX 8.25% _____

SHIPPING/HANDLING $ 3.50

TOTAL DUE _____ $ _____

Please allow two weeks for delivery

SHIP TO:
NAME _____
ADDRESS _____
CITY _____ STATE _____ ZIP _____
DAY PHONE (____) _____ EVE. PHONE (____) _____

PLEASE COPY AND SHARE WITH A FRIEND   – T H A N K Y O U !